FROM THE VIRGINIA WOOLF WRITERS' WORKSHOP

"The novelist," she observes in a very quiet, serious voice, "is terribly exposed to life. Taste, sound, movement, a few words here, a gesture there, a man coming in, a woman going out, even the motor that passes in the street or the beggar who shuffles along the pavement, and all the reds and blues and lights and shades of the scene claim his attention." Is this your sensibility? she asks. Are you attuned to the world around you? Taking in this, noticing that?

A true novelist, she continues, shaping one of her sea images, "can no more cease to receive impressions than a fish in mid-ocean can cease to let the water rush through his gills." But collecting impressions is not enough, she warns them. The true art of the writer is to sift through the rush of the impressions and cull out only the essential details.

THE Virginia Woolf
WRITERS' WORKSHOP

SEVEN LESSONS TO INSPIRE GREAT WRITING

DANELL JONES

BANTAM BOOKS

NEW YORK   LONDON   TORONTO   SYDNEY   AUCKLAND

THE VIRGINIA WOOLF WRITERS' WORKSHOP
A Bantam Book

PUBLISHING HISTORY
Bantam hardcover edition published October 2007
Bantam trade paperback edition / December 2008

Published by Bantam Dell
A Division of Random House, Inc.
New York, New York

Book design by Ellen Cipriano

See page 162 for permissions and credits.

Library of Congress Catalog Card Number: 2007021630

Bantam Books and the rooster colophon are
registered trademarks of Random House, Inc.

ISBN 978-0-553-38492-5

Printed in the United States of America
Published simultaneously in Canada

www.bantamdell.com

BVG   10 9 8 7 6 5 4 3 2 1

ACKNOWLEDGMENTS

This book could not have been written without the gifted Virginia Woolf scholars who have helped to make her works available and who have provided invaluable insight into her creative project. A special thanks to two of them—Anne Fernald and Ruth Webb—who took on the added burden of reading the manuscript. Anne provided feedback and encouragement early on. Ruth painstakingly read the final draft. Her generosity and insight are gifts I will cherish always. I would also like to thank Edward Mendelson, whose wisdom shaped my understanding of Woolf from the very beginning. With this book, as with all my other projects, Celia Maddox has been unfailingly generous with her time, intelligence, and imagination. She is a gifted teacher who instills confidence and nurtures creativity even as she shows what needs improvement. A special thanks, too, to Virginia Tranel, who has been a model of inspiration in so many ways. Thank you to Ken Egan, Mary Cregan, Sheila Ruble, and Francesca Lees, all of whom read drafts at various stages. Many thanks to my agent, Sterling Lord, for his gentle guidance and good cheer. I have also been exceedingly fortunate to work with my editor, Philip Rappaport, and his assistant, Nina Sassoon, at Bantam Dell. They have been everything a writer could wish for: insightful, supportive, and generous. I would also like to thank my mom and her husband, John, for their kindness and support. Finally, my most heartfelt thanks goes to my husband, Tim Lehman, whose generosity of heart, mind, and spirit sustains me daily.

CONTENTS

PREFACE ∽ 1

PRACTICING ∽ 9

WORKING ∽ 19

CREATING ∽ 29

WALKING ∽ 39

READING ∽ 45

PUBLISHING ∽ 55

DOUBTING ∽ 67

SUGGESTED FURTHER READING ∽ 77

Sparks ∽ 81

Fiction Sparks ∽ 84

Nonfiction Sparks ∽ 106

Poetry Sparks ∽ 120

CONTENTS

BIBLIOGRAPHY ✆ 131

NOTES ✆ 135

INDEX ✆ 157

PERMISSIONS ✆ 162

THE VIRGINIA WOOLF
WRITERS' WORKSHOP

PREFACE

How many of us have imagined what it would be like to sit down with a great writer to talk shop? If only we could share a pint or two with Shakespeare, spend an afternoon rambling the moors with the Brontës, or join Jane Austen in her sitting room for tea, perhaps we could find out how they wrote those plays, poems, and novels that have enraptured us all these years. And perhaps we could return home with a nugget of wisdom that would be exactly what we needed to help us write our own books.

It is our good fortune that Virginia Woolf's abundant body of work makes just such an imagined conversation possible. In addition to her many novels and stories, she left an extensive diary, thousands of letters, numerous notebooks, and dozens of brilliant essays. We are doubly lucky that in these works she often meditated on the art of writing, pondering what makes a good novel or poem, questioning what living conditions make it possible to create a work of art, and identifying the qualities that writers need to succeed at their craft. Many of the things

Woolf might say if we had the chance to meet her are scattered throughout her works.

The idea for this book came in one of those flashes of inspiration that grace writers from time to time. I was rummaging through Woolf's books, collecting the ideas I thought would be of interest to my creative writing students, when suddenly I had a vision of Virginia Woolf swanning into a lecture hall. She was wearing a slightly shabby lilac dress; her fingers were stained with purple ink. She leaned over the podium and in that famously deep, musical, almost electrifying voice said to the class, "So you want to write." Woolf teaching a writing workshop, I thought. What a playful way to present some of her ideas about writing, and at the same time, convey something of her life and her personality.

The classroom scenes in this book are purely works of imagination, but they have been inspired by many years of reading and studying Woolf's works. While none of us can know what is in another's mind, I hope my imagined version of Woolf's thoughts pays homage to the wit and wisdom that infuse her books. In order to reach a little closer to the real person, I have tried, as much as possible, to use her own words. As you read, you'll notice that I have put all of her original phrasing in quotation marks. These quotes come directly from her letters, essays, diaries, and novels. However, because I have selected passages from many books and woven them together in this fictional context, I've had to add transitions here and there in order to keep the conversation fluent. To see how Woolf used these quotations in their original context, simply turn to the back of the book. There each quotation is reprinted along with its source, making it easy for you to find the original essay or letter or diary entry from which it derives. I hope this leads you back to Woolf's works, because there you will get the richness of her ideas, the quickness of her wit, and the sharpness of her intelligence in their original context—a pleasure well worth pursuing!

The many accounts left by those who knew Woolf personally also make it possible to imagine what it would be like to have her teach a writing workshop. Two volumes of reminiscences recorded by her friends and acquaintances provide wonderful details about her life and her character. Who would not love to learn that Woolf was a talented bread baker; her house was cluttered with books and magazines; she loved lawn bowling, drank good coffee, and ate her meals from purple lusterware dishes? As we read the reminiscences, we realize the portrait taking shape is nothing like the neurotic-genius-teetering-on-the-edge-of-madness that seems to dominate so much of the popular imagination. The Virginia Woolf her friends remember was funny and kind and had a wild, hooting laugh. She was magical with children; she loved to tell fantastic stories. Aspiring authors remember her as a famous writer who didn't hoard her fame, but reached out to young writers, encouraging their ideas and publishing their books. The Virginia Woolf they remember impressed them with her unpretentiousness, her imagination, and her intellect. Above all, those who knew her best remembered her immense sense of gaiety.

A couple of accounts in particular make it easy to imagine

her out of her writing room at Monk's House and into a class-room. In one, her niece describes inviting Woolf up to Newnham College, Cambridge, to chat with students about books. Naturally, the young women were thrilled at the chance to meet this fa-mous writer. Despite Woolf's fame, her niece recalls how unas-suming she was, how interested in the young women's ideas, how eager to hear what they had to say. Her friendly, inquisitive manner, she recalls, drew them out of their shells and helped their ideas shine through their shyness. As I read this, my vision of Woolf as a teacher seemed justified.

But of course she wasn't a teacher. She had done a little vol-unteer teaching at a working men and women's college as a young woman, but she was never a member of a faculty, and she certainly never taught a writing workshop. Nevertheless, the several important lectures she gave about the art of writing do convey a clear sense of what she might have been like in front of a classroom. One thing I think we can be sure of: she would have been funny. Her wit dances across the pages of *A Room of One's Own* and "Professions for Women," two essays based on lectures she had delivered. There's little question that she would have brought that clever playfulness to the classroom. But she also would have taken the task of teaching people about writing very seriously. Her remarks to the class, despite flashes of whimsy, would leave no doubt that it was a topic she had considered profoundly.

But is it right to place the very British Woolf in that oh-so-American institution of the writers' workshop? To deposit her in one of those stuffy seminar rooms where aspiring writers meet with an established author to talk about writing, to try out new ideas, and to share their work? I think so and here's why: I can't help but believe that the best workshops share the spirit of creative companionship that was so important to Woolf and her friends. Like the Thursday evening get-togethers in Bloomsbury, the workshop offers the chance to talk to people who care about words; to push one's thinking a little further through intelligent conversation; to live, if only for a few hours, in a world that honors above all the well-turned phrase, the dazzle of imagination.

I hope these pages will be a creative introduction to Woolf's ideas that both the aspiring writer and the seasoned craftsperson will find inspiring. They may also be of interest to those who are simply curious about Woolf even if they don't mean to write themselves. It seems to me that all of us can learn a great deal from those who have gone before, especially those rare beings who have succeeded, as E. M. Forster said of Woolf, in pushing "the light of the English language a little further against darkness."

The book is organized into seven imaginary classroom sessions, each one focusing on a central theme important to Woolf's writing life. Woven into these chapters are her observations about a variety of genres, including fiction, poetry, biography, memoir, and the essay. At the end of each chapter there is a selection of "writing sparks," short activities designed to stimulate thinking about Woolf's ideas and to encourage writing. At the back of the book, you'll find dozens more fiction, poetry, and nonfiction exercises allowing further practice. I have also included the list of quotations and their sources mentioned above, as well as suggestions for further reading.

It is important to say that this book is not intended to turn out a passel of Virginia Woolf imitators. She honored, above all else, the artist's personal vision and always encouraged writers to embrace that vision no matter what. "To sacrifice a hair of the head of your vision, a shade of its colour," she says in *A Room of One's Own*, "in deference to some Headmaster with a silver pot in his hand or to some professor with a measuring-rod up his sleeve, is the most abject treachery." To that end, the exercises included here, while drawn from Woolf's work and ideas, do not so much invite imitation as experimentation. They are meant as warm-ups or tune-ups or sparks for the imagination, and have been designed to help writers practice their skills and gain insight into their own creative vision.

Woolf's advice about writing should also be taken in a similar vein. Her suggestions for reading widely, practicing one's scales, and keeping a regular writing routine offer a sound foundation for any writer's life. Other suggestions, like not publishing before thirty, should probably be taken in spirit—don't be in too much of a rush to publish—rather than as hard-and-fast rules. All writers must determine for themselves what advice to follow and what to dismiss. For better or worse, writers continually negotiate the space between trusting and challenging their teachers. Only they can decide when it is time to take guidance from their mentors and when they must strike out on their own, following their own instincts.

For me, one of the most vital lessons Woolf has to teach is

the importance of the creative life itself. Writers, she would say, live closer to reality than other people. They see the beauty of the world because they look at it closely, making a point of noticing intensely. Simply moving through the world with a writer's eye, she would contend, gives us a richer human experience, a more expansive life, whether we ever succeed at communicating our experiences in words or not.

I hope this book encourages writers in the way Woolf would have wanted: helping them to become more sensitive to the muscle and weight of language, and encouraging them to press on through every obstacle to seek their own creative visions. For the artist, I think she would say, not only creates her art, but is in turn created by it.

PRACTICING

WHAT, SHE WRITES ON THE board, are the conditions necessary to produce a work of art?

Up shoots the hand of a young woman in an Ani DiFranco T-shirt. "A room of her own and five hundred a year?"

True, she says, amazed how the words she wrote all those years ago seem to have sprouted wings and ascended on a flight of their own. But, she continues, trying to explain the idea behind the phrase, that is because a writer "wants life to proceed with the utmost quiet and regularity. He wants," she says, laying deliberate stress on each repetition, "to see the same faces, to read the same books, to do the same things day after day, month after month." The class rustles nervously. This sounds nothing like the glamorous life of a famous writer.

"So that nothing may disturb or disquiet," she continues, her voice growing low and musical, "the mysterious nosings about, feelings round, darts, dashes and sudden discoveries of that very shy and illusive spirit, the imagination." She pauses dramatically. Let that one sink in a bit, she decides.

"I hope I am not giving away professional secrets," she says provocatively, "if I say that a novelist's chief desire is to be as unconscious as possible."

"Unconscious?" a very tall young man asks with surprise.

"Imagine me," she instructs, "writing a novel in a state of trance." Think, she tells them, of the image of a "fisherman lying sunk in dreams on the verge of a deep lake with a rod held out over the water." As writers, we must try to clear our minds and let our "imagination sweep unchecked round every rock and cranny of the world that lies submerged in the depths of our unconscious being." She settles back in her seat and watches their faces. They are all so different: young, old; women, men; every race, color, and creed one could imagine. Not so long ago in England, she muses, writers tended to be men from well-to-do families educated at certain expensive universities. And now? Now these ordinary people—these commoners and outsiders—sit before her, eager to write. What exciting stories they will tell, she thinks.

The students are eager to learn more about her life, so she tells them that in fact she herself did the same thing day after day, month after month: she wrote. Typically, she explains, she worked every morning—seven days a week—from about nine-thirty to lunchtime. She smiles, remembering herself hunched down in a wicker chair sporting tattered overalls and steel-rimmed glasses, a writing board stretched across her lap, smoking home-rolled cigarettes and drafting out novels in purple ink. In those days, it seemed as if she perpetually wore a blossom of purple over her fingers.

She always jealously guarded her writing time, she tells them, carefully organizing her day so that her mornings were completely uninterrupted. No appointments, no visitors, no manuscript reviewing—just writing. She wants to show these students that they can produce a surprising amount of work if they carve out a time for writing each day and commit to it. It is amazing what you can get done, she says. She knows she has her strict schedule to thank for her own steady production. What did it add up to in the end? Some ten novels, dozens of short stories, hundreds of essays. The letters alone were in the thousands. And all those stacks of diaries and reading notes? More than sixty volumes, wasn't it? Oh, if she's honest with herself, she has to admit that the novels didn't come spilling out every day. Sometimes she felt no power of phrase making and would merely take notes or write little sketches to amuse herself. Still, they must be diligent, she tells them. Keep at it; you'll amaze yourself.

Yet writing, she warns them gravely, could be the easiest part of the task. Sticking to the routine when every force in the world will try to steal it—or try to make you feel excruciatingly guilty about wanting to write—can be much tougher. She must encourage them to resist the fierce emotional traps that will try to get in the way of their creative life. They must, especially if they are women, she warns, be prepared for a fight. They must even be prepared, she adds in a slow, solemn tone, to kill.

"Kill?" a plump woman asks, her anxious expression suggesting that she didn't expect murder to be a part of a writing program.

Yes, Woolf tells her. You must be prepared to kill a cruel, destructive creature named the Angel in the House. That selfless, giving caretaker, she explains, who always puts everyone else's needs ahead of her own; who thinks her own work is not important. Woolf admits that she had to kill her own Angel in the House.

"Had I not killed her," she warns them, "she would have killed me. She would have plucked the heart out of my writing." Several women in the class nod knowingly. But killing her, Woolf tells them, will not be easy.

"She died hard," Woolf says with all seriousness, and "she was always creeping back when I thought I had despatched her." Then she cocks her head slightly, a mischievous look stealing over her face and adds, of course, "her fictitious nature was of great assistance to her." She pauses slightly and declares killing her is essential if you are serious about protecting your time. Even then, she cautions, it can be a daily battle that you don't always win. "Such a good morning's writing I'd planned," she admits to them with a sigh, and then next thing I would know I'd "wasted the cream of my brain on the telephone."

"And you didn't even have cell phones back then," a student observes half incredulously.

This new millennium certainly has more than its share of diversions, Woolf reckons. But still, what a thrilling time to live. No wonder they all want to be writers. Yet given so many distractions, it becomes all the more necessary to remind them to preserve something just for themselves, their own private creative outlet. They each must, she tells them earnestly, keep a diary, a journal.

In the back of the room, a smartly dressed woman nervously raises her hand.

"But what are we supposed to do with it exactly? Do we write down how we feel about everything? Or is it some kind of record about what happens? I'm just not sure what you mean."

Use it as a writer, she advises. I often used my diary, she explains, to practice my scales and to experiment with creating different effects.

"What do you mean 'practice your scales'?" a young man sporting a crew cut asks.

I mean, she says her voice rising with enthusiasm, just write. Write "nonsense by the ream. Be silly, be sentimental, imitate Shelley; give the rein to every impulse; commit every fault of style, grammar, taste, and syntax; pour out; tumble over; loose anger, love, satire, in whatever words you can catch, coerce or create, in whatever metre, prose, poetry, or gibberish that comes to hand. Thus you will learn to write."

She goes on to tell them how she used her diary to practice specific skills. In it she rehearsed description, dialogue, even character development.

"The habit of writing thus for my own eye only," she says, was "good practice." She tells them how she used to sketch out scenes drawn from an actual experience—for instance, having tea with Thomas Hardy—in which she would try to capture the tone, the mood, and the setting of the afternoon as well as the charming idiosyncrasy of the aging novelist. These scales, she tells them, are a great way to limber up the mind and keep the eye sharp.

She also acknowledges that when she wasn't writing well—and sometimes even when she was—she would turn to her diary to complain, to scold, or to have a laugh, sometimes at other people's expense, she admits sheepishly, remembering some of her more wicked entries. It is a place she liked to use to doodle around, to be lazy, or crabby. In your journal, she emphasizes, let yourself play, free from the burden of the perfect sentence or the perfect idea.

"And you kept it every single day, religiously?" the smartly dressed woman asks.

Follow your own sensibility, she advises. Write regularly, but as it suits you. You can write in it every day if you like, or do as I did, and just write consistently, every day or two. I would have a burst of entries in a row, she explains, and then a gap of several days and then another burst. That suited my creativity. Find your own rhythm and follow it.

Especially when you are learning, she cautions, try not to take writing too seriously. The conviction that every word has to be perfect more often produces paralysis than good writing. She tells them that playing around with a few sketches—doing their scales—lets them try something new when there's nothing at stake. Don't censor your work, she says gently; just write even if you struggle here and stumble there. And it doesn't matter in the least whether a journal entry ever leads to anything. Its purpose is simply to sharpen the eye and ear or to warm up the mind for writing.

And yet sometimes they might find that scales do lead to discoveries and insights. She remembers how ideas for novels used to come rushing in as she was writing in her diary. Playing, experimenting, might lead to stories or poems, she assures them, or might reveal a new direction for a work in progress. But remember, she repeats, such exercises only keep their delicious power when not taken too seriously, when treated simply as a game.

If they decide to peek into her diaries after class—they've all been published now, she remembers with mixed emotions—they will also make another important discovery. They will soon realize how she experienced the same roller coaster of emotion that they experience, that every writer experiences. In the diaries, they will see entries where she vents her frustration at writing badly. She remembers some of her harsh admonishments. "It is a disgrace," she scolded herself, "that I write nothing, or if I write, write sloppily." They will also see the passages of self-criticism, when she would see a weakness in her work and try to remedy it. "I must learn to write more succinctly," she would remind herself. "I am horrified by my own looseness." And then, with some relief, she recalls the passages that show the glorious pleasure of a work spilling out almost effortlessly. "I am now writing as fast and freely as I have written in the whole of my life," she remembers scribbling in her diary while composing *To the Lighthouse*, "more so—20 times more so—than any novel yet." Of course, they will see, too, the in-between. "I do feel fairly sure that I am grazing as near as I can to my own ideas, and getting a tolerable shape for them," she recorded while creating *Mrs. Dalloway*, "but I have my ups and downs." She kept the diaries entirely for herself, she knows, but it doesn't seem like it would hurt for these aspiring writers to have a peek now and then. Perhaps they will find something of use, even if it is only to see someone else's questions, someone else's struggles.

Ultimately, she tells them, her own diary testifies to the incredible power of a regular writing practice, the power of doing the same things day after day, month after month. For those who want to write, she reminds them gently, a commitment to writing on a daily basis ensures one essential thing: that you will be there when that very shy and very illusive spirit showers you with the gift of words.

 *W*riting *S*parks

I. Write an obituary for your own Angel in the House. Take the time to describe her (did she, for example, soar around the house pointing out all the dust or expect a three-course meal each evening?). Explain why you killed her, how she died (holding up a can of cleanser? scolding you in your mother's voice?), and why no one will miss her. If necessary, include a plan for killing her again if she attempts a resurrection.

2. Buy yourself a notebook to use as a journal. It doesn't matter if it is fancy or plain, if the pages are lined or unlined. The important thing is that you feel that you can write anything in it. Also buy yourself a special pen. Woolf loved to write with purple ink. What color would you choose? Remember—and this is important—this pen is for your personal use only. The Angel is dead: you don't have to share.

3. Commit to fifteen minutes a day to sit with your journal and let yourself play with words. Vent, describe, ruminate, celebrate. Record quotations that move you; paste images that inspire you. Give yourself the gift of fifteen minutes of creative playtime every day.

4. If you seem to have trouble preserving fifteen minutes a day for yourself, your Angel in the House is alive and well. Kill her off—or at least slow her down—with this series of exercises:

    a. The next time you open your journal, list the things you do instead of writing. For example, do you watch TV? Talk on the phone? Type your child's/boyfriend's/roommate's homework?

    b. Now explain to yourself why you let other things come before your writing time.

    c. In your next entry, imagine what you could do

differently. What would happen if you said no to a request? Or if you cut short another activity by fifteen minutes? Imagine the scene in detail. Include dialogue. Make yourself invincible.

d. Finally, use your journal to describe all the things you'd like to write about. Make a list of all those exciting ideas that have been piling up in your brain. Then, when you come back to the book, use that list as a jumping-off place.

5. Let yourself write badly. Virginia Woolf tells us that's the only way to learn. Write reminders to yourself to hang up in your writing area or to tape to your notebook. For example, "The great writing goddess Virginia Woolf authorizes me to write nonsense by the ream" or "I am free to commit every fault of style, grammar, taste, and syntax. Virginia Woolf says so."

WORKING

"And what about this room of one's own and five hundred a year?" a woman in the back of the room asks at the start of the next session.

"Yeah," another person adds, "and how much is that in dollars anyway?"

Well, Woolf begins, but before she can explain a balding man intently focused on a piece of scrap paper interrupts.

"As far as I can tell," he says, scribbling down numbers as he speaks, "accounting for inflation, variation of living standards, income tax, a fluctuating exchange rate, and so forth, five hundred pounds in 1929 would be somewhere around the national median salary these days in the U.S. and Britain. Let's say about thirty-six thousand dollars."

They take things so literally, Woolf muses, when what I really meant was enough money to have a quiet room, to have time to think, maybe to travel a bit.

"But you were lucky," a young woman in dreadlocks protests. "You had an aunt who was thrown from her horse in

Bombay and left you five hundred a year. What if we have no aunt to leave us an inheritance?"

Indeed, she tells them, she did have an aunt who left her a little money, even if that aunt was not named Mary Beton, as she teasingly claimed in *A Room of One's Own,* and did not live in Bombay, and never fell from her horse; in fact, she was a rather retiring sort who lived a nunnish life in Cambridge. She didn't even, as it turns out, leave Woolf five hundred a year. Those were merely imaginative facts, she tells them, designed to create a certain impression, to have a certain effect, in that playful essay. For you see, she tells them with mocking seriousness, "I prefer, where truth is important, to write fiction."

But they are right, she did have an inheritance. And it did provide her a regular income, if not quite enough to live on. She admits she was lucky to be born into a family of means. Still, even though they left her money, her family didn't provide her with a university education as they did for her brothers. She was not sent to Cambridge as they were to prepare for a profession. But thanks to the work of Aphra Behn in the seventeenth century, she tells them, she could earn money by her wits.

Think of Aphra Behn, Woolf cries out with passion.

"Aphra who?" someone asks.

Aphra Behn, England's first woman novelist, she announces. "Mrs. Behn was a middle-class woman forced by the death of her husband and," she adds with a wry grin, "some unfortunate adventures of her own to make her living by her wits." She took to writing and she made a living.

"But why is some woman from the seventeenth century important to us?" someone asks.

Because, Woolf declares, for the first time in history women could think about writing as a profession. They could seriously consider the possibility of writing for a living. Of course, not a few parents of that time (and for a long time after) would have rather seen their daughters dead than writers of plays and novels. Still, it was the beginning. Aphra Behn made it possible for any of us to work very hard and earn five hundred a year with our pens.

"But you were a famous novelist. Of course you made money from your pen," a young man observes from the back row.

Ah, but what they don't realize, she tells them, is that she had written at least five novels and was as old as the hills (in her midforties to be exact) by the time she started making money from her fiction. Before that, she wrote articles and reviews in order to balance her checkbook.

"Well, then," a man sitting near her right elbow asks, "how did you get started?"

As a young woman, she tells them, she wrote from ten in the morning until one in the afternoon. She wrote an article and sent it to a magazine. A month later, the editor of that magazine sent her a check.

"A very glorious day it was for me," she tells them as if—in spite of the fact that she is now famous—she still feels the thrill of turning words into coins. And beneath her words the students also hear her saying that she knows what they are going through. She, too, has been a beginner. She, too, has doubted. But she has worked and triumphed. And they can work and triumph, too.

As she goes on, a hint of mischief mixes with the British refinement. About that money, "I have to admit that instead of spending that sum upon bread and butter, rent, shoes and stockings, or butcher's bills, I went out and bought a cat—a beautiful cat, a Persian cat." She pauses and then adds with a mocking smile, "which very soon involved me in bitter disputes with my neighbours."

Leaning back in her chair, she tilts her head and laughs in a boundless, delightful, almost hooting way.

"What," she says teasingly, "could be easier than to write articles and to buy Persian cats with the profits?"

And what would you say, she asks them, if I told you my very first paid review was for the women's supplement of a religious newspaper? Not something she would have chosen, she admits, but it got her started.

"And how did you get that assignment?" the young woman asks.

The way so many people get jobs even today: a friend had a friend who needed someone to write a book review for the women's pages of her church paper. So, I say, don't be afraid to ask your friends for help even if they are not literary. You may be surprised what you get. And if your first opportunity isn't what you expected, don't worry. Start where you can and discover where it leads you.

"What was your attitude about having to do journalism to make ends meet? Didn't you think it was beneath you?" a very dignified elderly gentleman asks.

Oh no, she tells them, although one friend of mine tried to convince me that writing for the likes of *Vogue* magazine was demeaning to my art and would injure my prestige. Of course, I told him he was ridiculous and that my writing would not suffer for being printed in the pages of a popular women's magazine. Besides, I liked the money, she laughs. True, she admits, she did her share of grousing about deadlines, dull topics, and narrow-minded editors. But she realizes now that writing journalism was one of the ways she learned her craft. Writing reviews for magazines and newspapers taught her to write concise, lively prose. And she'd learned how to read well, too—closely and intensely. She had to figure out how to review every kind of book imaginable, from novels and poetry to history and memoir. At her busiest, she'd written nearly fifty a year. No, she sighs, journalism was a good education for a novelist.

So you see, she assures them, she knows what it is to earn by one's wits. The money's of consequence, to be sure, but the greatest reward comes from the sense of power, of freedom.

And that was her point, she explains, about the five hundred a year.

When I say five hundred pounds and a room of one's own, I really mean "the habit of freedom and the courage to write exactly what we think.... Even allowing a generous margin for symbolism, that five hundred a year stands for the power to contemplate, that lock on the door means the power to think for oneself."

But of course a real lock doesn't hurt either, she laughs. Symbolism aside, it is important sometimes to have a real room with a real door. The interruptions can undo you.

From her earliest days of independence, she informs them, she resolved to have her own working space. She thinks back to those early days in Bloomsbury, the house in Gordon Square she shared with her siblings after her parents had died. She recalls how she and her sister Vanessa fiercely guarded their working routines, each claiming a room to use as her studio. Vanessa the painter; Virginia the writer. How she envied Vanessa at her easel, so upright, so dignified. Woolf smiles to herself as she remembers how she tried to assume something of her sister's composure by setting up a very tall table in her room where she could write standing up. She can almost see her young gangly self standing for two or three hours at a time writing. It was exhausting, but wonderful.

One of the most important writing spaces of her life, she confesses to her students, wasn't half so grand as all that. She tells them how she worked in an overflowing stockroom in the basement of her home in Tavistock Square, London. Right down the hall was the hustle and bustle of the Hogarth Press, the publishing company she and her husband started. She liked to hole up at a big desk in one of the large stockrooms, rather enjoying the ever-shifting mountain of books heaped around her. Her desk, she admits, was always a mess of half-written stories, letters, and notes piled helter-skelter. The entire ambience of the room, her husband used to say, was one of utter disarray. But tidiness was never of particular concern to her, she knows all too well. So, she advises them, take whatever space you can get—as long as it serves you. You needn't build an extra wing on the house or spend a lot of money. All you need are privacy and whatever degree of comfort feeds your creativity.

Of course, she acknowledges, once they could afford it, they made a few changes. At their country home, Monk's House, down in Sussex, her husband turned an old tool shed in the garden into a writing room for her. She loved writing in her little room with French doors and big windows looking out across the Sussex downs. She loved her writing desk; loved vases filled with flowers from her husband's garden. It was a room of warmth and light; the creative sanctuary she visited daily; a room of one's own in its most idealized form.

"It's been preserved by the British National Trust," one of the older women in the class remarks. "My husband and I visited it last year when we were on vacation."

The National Trust? she says. My house, a tourist stop?

The students nod.

Will others now write half mockingly, half admiringly of visiting her house, she wonders, as she had written of her excursions to the homes of other writers? She supposes it no small irony that one of the very first pieces she ever published was about her visit to the Brontë parsonage. She is quite sure she'd said something slightly irreverent about Charlotte's dress, or was it about Emily's dog?

"Didn't you once say that you thought writers had an

uncanny ability for housing themselves in the way we imagine they would—or something like that?" the woman in black asks.

"A faculty for housing themselves appropriately, for making the table, the chair, the curtain, the carpet into their own image?" she says bowing her head, blushing slightly. Yes, I believe I did. Perhaps, she thinks to herself, she owes an apology to Dickens and Keats and the Carlyles for the things she'd said about visiting their houses, too.

Well, she decides, she can live with people tramping about her house, eyeing her things, and imagining that they know her, just as long as they don't canonize her. She couldn't bear to have them do to her what they did to poor old Rupert Brooke after he died in the Great War—turn him into some kind of shiny, immaculate, sentimental hero, no good to anyone. Visit my house, she tells them, walk in my garden, look at the books; you can even turn them over in your hand or run your fingers along their binding. But, she implores, please don't entomb me, no matter how nobly.

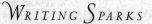

WRITING SPARKS

1. Find a place in your home and create a space of your own. While it need not be an entire room, it should be someplace where you are comfortable and have a degree of privacy. A comfy chair in the bedroom or a

bean bag tucked in the corner of the back porch will do. You don't need anything fancy: remember, Woolf glued an ink pot to a board and laid it across her lap in a crowded stockroom. Do take a little time to make the area yours by putting up inspiring pictures, quotations, and the like. Use fabric to create a little privacy tent if that appeals to you. You can get Japanese-style screens to use as a room divider as well. They come in many different styles and sizes. Once your space is set up, write a curse and post it nearby. Make your curse very clear and vivid; it should indicate that this is your private space and identify—in gory detail—what terrible things will happen to anyone who violates it.

2. In an essay called "Street Haunting," Woolf contemplates the ways in which our rooms reveal who we are. All the objects we collect in our rooms express our personalities and carry with them powerful memories. Write an emotional survey of your room, identifying what various objects reveal about your personality. Take special care to show how your objects reflect your interesting quirks, how they represent your view of life, your basic values.

3. Woolf wrote in her essay "The London Scene" that we can learn about great writers by visiting their homes and getting an idea how they lived. Find a famous person's house near you; if you are lucky enough to visit the home of a famous writer, all the

better. Visit the house, closely observing as much as you can. Take note of the setting, the size, the furniture, the household objects, the library, the art, and anything else that catches your fancy. Ask yourself what it is about a famous person's home that increases your sense of intimacy. Now write an essay about visiting this house. Include at least one scene where you imagine the famous person doing something in one of the rooms you've visited. Incorporate the objects you've observed as you describe the action. Let the scene not only show the room but reveal something of the famous person's character. Read Woolf's essays "Haworth, November 1904" and "Great Men's Houses" for inspiration.

4. Long before Woolf became a best-selling novelist, she wrote reviews and articles to make ends meet. She knew what it meant to write a certain number of words aimed at a general audience and how to meet a deadline. These days, we are surrounded by lots of publications: newsletters, alumni magazines, free presses, gazillions of Web sites. Identify one that is of interest to you and write an article that you could imagine being published there. Make sure you have a good sense of the appropriate audience as well as style and length. If you ever decide to contact them about a possible writing assignment, you can use your article as a sample of your work.

CREATING

For next time, she says at the end of the session, please prepare a little something to share with the class.

An uneasy silence smothers the room until an earnest young man in the front finally blurts out a question.

"What do you want us to write?"

Woolf looks rather startled by his question.

"So long as you write what you wish to write, that is all that matters."

"But what do you want?" the woman next to him echoes, twirling her long hair nervously around an index finger.

Woolf sits back in her chair. "Write exactly as you think— that is the only way," she wants to say. But perhaps they would understand it better if she described a kind of experience, a kind of sensation.

"Examine for a moment an ordinary mind on an ordinary day," she begins. "The mind receives a myriad impressions— trivial, fantastic, evanescent, or engraved with the sharpness of steel. Let us," she continues, "record the atoms as they fall upon the mind in the order in which they fall, let us trace the pattern."

"So you're saying we have to write stream of consciousness, then?" the young man asks.

How could I possibly tell you, a young man with a mind of his own, what to write? she wonders.

What I'm saying is that "writers are infinitely sensitive; each writer has a different sensibility." Just as we each perceive the world according to our capacity, she wants to tell them, so, too, we must write according to our vision. But we cannot do that unless we resolve to be true to ourselves and not imitators of others.

"But," the girl with her hair around her finger implores, "what pattern do you want us to use? Exposition, rising action, complication, climax, resolution? Or what?"

Oh dear, Woolf thinks. She didn't realize they were as browbeaten as all that.

Let me ask you a question, she says, raising her long, elegant hand into the air. "Sometimes at country fairs you may have seen a professor on a platform exhorting the peasants to come up and buy his wonder-working pills." The older students nod their heads yes.

"Does she mean like the professor in *The Wizard of Oz*?" one of the younger students asks the older man next to her.

"Yes," he whispers back. "Professor Marvel."

"Whatever their disease," Woolf continues, "whether of body or mind, he has a name for it and a cure." Am I right? she asks.

The class registers general agreement.

"And if they hang back in doubt he whips out a diagram and points with a stick at different parts of the human anatomy, and gabbles so quickly such long Latin words that first one shyly stumbles forward and then another, and takes his bolus and carries it away and unwraps it secretly and swallows it in hope." Her students begin to smile now, amused by the image of the country hicks lined up at the feet of a quack for their wonder pills.

Well, she tells them, shrugging her shoulders slightly, there are some writing teachers, "professors" of fiction, she says with a delicious scorn in her voice, who prescribe a similar treatment for writers.

Aspiring writers come forward, she says adopting a mock heroic attitude, "and receive five pills together with nine suggestions for home treatment. In other words they are given five 'review questions' to answer and are advised to read nine books or parts of books." The professor asks them to define realism and define romance and then define the difference between realism and romance. Then he demands to know the benefits of using "the realistic method." Realistic method, indeed, she huffs.

I have no doubt, she continues, that such a professor has "a bundle of testimonials to the miraculous nature of his cures. But let us consider: we are not credulous ploughboys; and fiction," she adds, tilting her chin downward and fixing her eyes on the class, "is not a disease." She pauses, her face broadening with a mocking grin.

In fact, she continues, barely able to contain her laughter, "in England we have been in the habit of saying that fiction is an art." She lets out a loud, unselfconscious hoot of a laugh.

Once she's gathered herself, she goes on more seriously. Now according to some of these teachers, she explains, "every work of art can be taken to pieces, and those pieces can be named and numbered, divided and subdivided, and given their order of precedence, like the internal organs of a frog." Such teachers tell us each story must have, she says with a note of exasperation in her voice, "the complication, the major knot, and the explication." And then they go on to talk about something they like to call emphasis. "Emphasis by terminal position, by initial position, by pause, by direct proportion." She halts to catch her breath. And if we just learn all the names of all the pieces and where they go, if we just learn to dissect our frog and put it back together again, then, they say, we will be able to write.

She shakes her head incredulously.

"You may dissect your frog," she advises them solemnly, "but you cannot make it hop." I am quite sure, she says, settling back in the wooden chair at the head of the table, even the credulous ploughboy knows that. She scans the room, looking at each eager face. She knows what she must say to them. There is a simple truth she must share.

"Nobody knows anything about the laws of fiction. We can only trust our instincts. Any method is right, every method is right, that expresses what we wish to express, if we are writers. No 'method,' no experiment, even of the wildest—is forbidden."

Remember this, she tells them, her voice glowing, "be truthful, and the result is bound to be amazingly interesting."

She takes a minute to remind them that she spent her life experimenting with all kinds of forms and styles. And the truth is, she tells them, it was her more conventional novels—*Orlando, Flush,* and *The Years*—that turned her into a best-selling author, not the experimental works so popular now like *Mrs. Dalloway, The Waves,* or *To the Lighthouse.* No one really knows what will last, she tells them. So why limit yourself to satisfy someone else's idea of a good book? Of course, she admits, she has always loved playing with language and has always been particularly critical of novels that seemed to her overly formulaic.

But more than anything, she tells them, she has valued expansiveness. She encourages them to embrace their particular vision without worrying "whether it matters for ages or only for hours." It is treachery of the vilest kind, she warns, to conform to someone else's idea of good writing. "It is much more important," she insists, "to be oneself than anything else."

But, she adds, she cannot advocate creative freedom at the expense of critical judgment. "Write daily; write freely," she advises, "but let us always compare what we have written with what the great writers have written." She knows all too well that this part of the assignment is not always pleasant. "It is humiliating," she admits, "but it is essential."

Learn suspense, she suggests, by noting the shrewd turns of Jane Austen's dialogue. Discover psychological intricacy from John Donne's poetry. From Thomas Hardy, see how to develop characters who are both intensely individual and yet reverberate with symbolic meaning. Go to Charlotte Brontë for speed, color, and strength. To Thoreau for revealing the natural world with passionate intensity. And by all means read Shakespeare. Read Shakespeare, she says, for everything: his incandescence, his speed, his word-coining power, and especially for a glimpse of a mind that seemed to be able to compose utterly without impediment.

In other words, she advises, improve your craft by learning from great writers, both living and dead. She never found formal reviews by other writers in newspapers and magazines very helpful to her own writing, she confesses. And what good are reviews, she asks, if they do not help writers improve their work? There is much to approve of, she observes, in these writing programs and workshops that abound today. In her day, in fact, she proposed a system that had much in common with today's writers' workshops. Why not abolish formal reviews, she had proposed then, and develop a system in which professional writers (whose qualifications would be the books they'd written) would meet with other writers in private consultation like doctors and their patients?

"The writer then would submit his work to the judge of his choice," she explains, "an appointment would be made; an interview arranged. In strict privacy, and with some formality— the fee, however, would be enough to ensure that the interview did not degenerate into tea-table gossip—doctor and writer would meet; and for an hour they would consult upon the book in question. They would talk, seriously and privately." This privacy would allow both "doctor" and writer to talk openly, she affirms, and to concentrate on the book without worrying about the reading public or book sales. The writer would have the chance to ask questions, to describe what he or she was trying to accomplish, and to tap "a well-stored mind, housing other books and even other literatures."

And it is not just beginning writers who would profit from such a system, she acknowledges. "The art of writing is difficult," she asserts, and "at every stage the opinion of an impersonal and disinterested critic would be of the highest value."

"Who would not," she asks them, a smile spreading over her face, "spout the family teapot in order to talk with Keats for an hour about poetry, or with Jane Austen about the art of fiction?"

She can see from the faraway looks on their faces that in their minds they have already begun their walking tour with Keats, have already joined Jane Austen in the sitting room.

Bring something for next time, she reminds them gently as they begin to drift out of the room. And don't forget, she cries out as they shuffle slowly down the narrow hallway, record the atoms as they fall.

WRITING SPARKS

1. Jot down any "rules" you've learned about writing. They can be anything from "always capitalize at the beginning of a sentence" to "develop a clear setting as soon as possible in a story." Select one of the rules—the one you like best or the one you like least—and violate it. Write a poem, story, or essay—whichever you like—without using capital letters. Or create a scene without a setting. The idea here is to think about rules and what happens, good and bad, when you challenge them.

2. Sit in a quiet place for five or ten minutes. As you sit, try to be aware of the thoughts, images, and sensations moving through your mind. Be alert to abrupt shifts and unexpected juxtapositions. Then, as best you can, take up your pen or tap at your computer keys and try to trace the pattern of the impressions as they showered over you. Try to imitate in words the shifts and jumps of your thoughts. Don't censor yourself. Allow changes in tense, abrupt disconnections, nonsensical phrasing.

3. Give yourself permission to experiment with style. Tell the story of Little Red Riding Hood (or any favorite short tale) using long, meandering phrases and

opulently poetic language. The following day, write another version of the story using short, spare, concise language. Notice how word choice as well as sentence length and sentence complexity can change the tone and feeling of the story. Does one version appeal to you more than the other? Does it capture your idea of the story more fully, more precisely? Why?

4. Woolf was famous for her formal experiments, especially for her use of a stream-of-consciousness technique. In stream-of-consciousness narratives, we are thrust into the moving current of a character's thoughts, feelings, and sensory perceptions. Bits of dreams or fantasies sometimes swirl around with perceptions of the outside world. Write the story of the Three Little Pigs using a stream-of-consciousness style.

5. Just for a change, now write the Three Little Pigs story with as little description of the characters' thoughts, ideas, and emotions as possible. Focus on the details of the physical world. Describe the setting and the characters' outward appearances; show us the characters' actions and give us their words. Resist the temptation to reveal their thoughts or emotional reactions.

WALKING

Woolf strides to the front of the room. She pulls an unremarkable lead pencil from the pocket of her sweater and holds it up into the air so everyone in the room can see it.

Sometimes one finds oneself feeling, she declares "passionately towards a lead pencil."

Her students' eyes narrow, unconvinced.

For, she continues, it is "under cover of this excuse we could indulge safely in the greatest pleasure of town life in winter—rambling the streets of London." She smiles widely as she explains how she has always loved street-rambling, finding it thrilling to be "part of that vast republican army of anonymous trampers." What greater pleasure is there than wandering the streets amid the roar of the city, the jostle of the people, and the musical sounds of urban life?

"What does that have to do with writing?" a young man asks rather too brusquely.

With writing? she repeats. Why, it has everything to do with writing. She settles into her chair at the head of the table. A ray of light filters in through the window creating a warm glow in the room. I like walking the city streets, she tells them, and I like "walking through the long grass in the meadows, the silver sheep clustering; & the downs soaring. It feeds me, rests me, satisfies me, as nothing else does." Walking, she confides, "has a holiness." Three women on her left surrender to the idea, their eyes growing dreamy. But the young man will not be content.

"But it's not very practical. Shouldn't we be spending that time writing instead of wandering around? I don't see the point."

Woolf tucks her long, thin hand under her chin and explains how she saw her time walking as part—a crucial part, in fact—of her creative time. Ah, she tells them, how many books and scenes and lectures she invented on those walks. You should have seen me sometimes, she muses, wandering the streets making up stories.

"I have been in such a haze and dream and intoxication, declaiming phrases, seeing scenes, as I walk," she says, smiling as the memory of those reveries flood back.

Use walking, she advises them, to snap out of drowsiness and to get your mind "in fine writing trim." It soothes. It clears the head. And once the mind is clear, how the images rush in. Sometimes she would walk for hours, inventing her books, observing the world.

But walking, she tells them, should also remind us of an essential, archetypal type of story. Think of Homer's *Odyssey*, she

says. Or James Joyce's *Ulysses.* Or even her own *Mrs. Dalloway.*
These are fundamental stories of travel, of journeys. She reminds them how *Mrs. Dalloway* takes place on a single day, and
how her characters travel around London on intersecting journeys. She used a similar technique in *A Room of One's Own.* Think
back to that essay, she tells them, and remember how she let the
paths and buildings of Oxbridge act as a kind of foil for her ru-
minating narrator. There's something to be said, she continues,
for moving your characters through remarkable landscapes. She
wonders if any of them noticed how in *Mrs. Dalloway* she created scenes beneath famous statues: the scandalous Achilles, the
doomed Charles George Gordon. Well, no need to go into that,
she thinks. They'll find their own way through their own cities.

She's always liked to walk daily regardless of weather, she
admits.

I used to walk "nosing along, making up phrases," she tells
them, on wet, windy days and warm sunny days. On my walks,
I felt I had "space to spread my mind out." How she loved her
country walks, watching the light play against the downs and always on the lookout for wild creatures.

How I loved to ramble through the downs with my dog
Pinka—in spite of the ugly suburban housing being thrown up
at that time, I still thought Sussex "the loveliest country in the
world, with the corn ripening, and yellow butterflies." Thinking
of sweet Pinka, her little spaniel, she feels her heart twinging.

But, no, she thinks, she will not talk of Pinka. She will just
tell them to take their daily walks. For the good of their hearts,

for the good of their writing. The writer needs time to think, she tells them, to muse, to rejuvenate, to spread out the mind.

Beat the drowse, make your brain hum, she tells them brightly, take a walk.

Writing Sparks

1. Use walking as a transition from work and family obligations to writing. If you are feeling too frazzled to work, resist plopping down in front of the TV and take a walk instead. Observe the world around you. Mentally note the sounds and colors and smells of your neighborhood. When you return, spend ten minutes with your notebook describing what you have encountered. Are there images that could find their way into a poem? An interaction or snippet of conversation that could spark a story? Read some entries in Woolf's *A Writer's Diary* for inspiration.

2. One of Woolf's favorite games was to watch people and create imaginary lives for them. Try playing this game alone or with a friend. Sit in a public place and take turns making up stories about the people who pass. Is that little old woman with the grocery sack a former Miss America? The man in plaid a compulsive

gambler? Just for fun, let your imagination run from the plausible to the outlandish.

3. When you find yourself erasing more than writing, take yourself for a spin around the block. As you walk, think about the problem you're trying to work out. Let yourself experiment as you wander through the open air. Tucking a pen and scrap of paper in your pocket can be helpful in case you have a break-through.

4. Write a short story or a poem whose main character uses the need to buy an insignificant object like a pencil as an excuse for rambling the streets of his or her hometown. Let the sights, sounds, tastes, and textures of the place invade your character's thoughts. Don't be afraid to let her interact with the world or even, perhaps, to get into a little trouble. By the end of the story, the place should function almost as another character in the piece. See Woolf's essay "Street Haunting" for ideas.

5. Tales about journeys are one of the oldest kinds of stories. Think, for example, of Odysseus's ten-year voyage to return to his wife after the Trojan War, or Leopold Bloom's stroll through Dublin, or Clarissa Dalloway's meandering through London. Write a story structured around a journey. It may be a big journey to an exotic land, such as the transatlantic voyage in Woolf's first novel, *The Voyage Out,* or a more

limited excursion such as Clarissa Dalloway's travels through her beloved metropolis. It may be as long or as short as you wish, but let the parts of the journey—beginning, middle, and end—create the structure of your story.

READING

AFTER A FEW SESSIONS, STUDENTS begin to notice that Woolf arrives at each class meeting with a new stash of books under her arm. It's always a jumble of works: Aeschylus, Shakespeare, and Dante mixed with newly minted biography, memoir, and history.

"Are you going to give us some advice about what authors to read?" a young man sporting owlish glasses inquires.

"The only advice that one person can give another about reading," she tells him, "is to take no advice."

"No advice?"

None whatsoever.

"But why?" he asks.

I can only tell you "to follow your own instincts," she advises him, "to use your own reason, to come to your own conclusions." You must embrace, she says, her voice warming with conviction, your "independence which is the most important quality that a reader can possess." She surveys the faces in the room. "Each of us," she reminds them, "has an appetite that must find for itself the food that nourishes it. Reading omnivorously, simultaneously, poems, plays, novels, histories, biographies, the old and the new," that is the only way to find the books that nurture us, that inspire us, that help us grow.

She tells them she learned this free-ranging philosophy of reading from her father, the distinguished Victorian man of letters Leslie Stephen. You see, she says quietly, she didn't go to school. She was educated at home, first by her mother, and then after she died, by her father. He was the one who gave her the run of his excellent library, encouraging her to read according to her taste. And it was in his library that she began reading voraciously: Shelley, Austen, Macaulay, Pepys, Coleridge, the Brontës, and Shakespeare. "Devouring books, almost faster than I like," her father had said with a kind of fastidious pride. He would let her choose her books freely, even though he hinted there might be some that were not entirely suited to a girl of fifteen. When she had finished reading, she recalls, they would sit down together. The old Victorian with his long gray beard would sit across from his slender daughter with the bright eyes and ask with a kind of seriousness that made her love him, what did you make of it?

"She takes in a great deal," he had told her mother, "& will really be an author in time." Woolf turns over this memory in her mind. Mingled with a lingering irritation at his all-consuming egotism is this iridescent gem of praise. It surprises her how it still sparkles.

"Let us bear in mind a piece of advice that an eminent

Victorian who was also an eminent pedestrian," and—she smiles—who happened to be my father, "once gave to walkers: 'Whenever you see a board up with "Trespassers will be prosecuted," trespass at once.' Literature is no one's private ground; literature is common ground."

"Nor let us," she says holding up a copy of *King Lear*, "shy away from the kings because we are commoners." She advises them to go to the library, get copies of Aeschylus, Shakespeare, Dante, and Virgil. These are writers for everyone, she explains, not just for professors in ivory towers. "Read me, read me for yourselves," they say. Read deeply and widely in the classics. But don't assume that you should limit yourself only to great books, she warns.

"A love of literature is often roused and nourished not by the good books," she acknowledges playfully, "but by the bad." Love your "rubbish reading," she declares, especially memoirs, biographies, and autobiographies, rich books that divulge the details of ordinary life, full of descriptions of how people live, their food, their clothes, their dreams, and their love lives. How exciting, she says, this ephemera of life; how dazzling in its way, like tiny shells scattered over a wide beach.

Who knows, she speculates, perhaps you will be inspired to sift through the moments of your life and find the lasting truths about yourself. Perhaps you will be inspired to write your own memoir one day. Of course, she had thought the 1930s were the great age for writing one's story.

At that time, she jokes, hardly anyone "reached the age of

thirty without writing his autobiography." But seeing the flood of memoirs now, the outpouring of her own time seems closer to a trickle.

"What," a tall, gray-haired woman asks, "makes a good memoir? I mean," she stammers self-consciously, "if we wanted to try to write our own?"

There is a secret, she warns them, to writing memoir, to writing one's own story. It is dark, she whispers, and perhaps a bit dirty.

The best memoirists tell the unpleasant truths, not only the flattering truths, she says gravely. If you think this is easy, "consider how difficult it is to tell the truth about oneself. To admit that one is petty, vain, mean, frustrated, tortured, unfaithful, and unsuccessful."

"You must illumine your own soul with its profundities and its shallows, and its vanities and its generosities, and say what your beauty means to you or your plainness," if you are to write a good autobiography. She observes them wistfully. The key, she reminds them, is to reveal themselves. It is not enough to describe the world around you if you offer no insight about the truths inside you.

In this, she acknowledges, memoir shares much with its cousin, the essay. Essay writing is a beautiful art, but full of perils, she warns.

"What do you mean?" someone asks.

For its backbone, she says, gazing above her as if the skeleton of a giant leviathan were suspended from the light fixtures, the essay has "some fierce attachment to an idea. It is on the back of an idea, something believed in with conviction or seen with precision," that the great essayists build their vision. That passion, that conviction, must be the source, must be the engine for the essay. As for the form, that is perhaps trickier.

The essay, she declares at the risk of being too metaphorical, "must be pure—pure like water or pure like wine, but pure from dullness, deadness, and deposits of extraneous matter." The essay, after all, is perhaps one of the most magical, if ephemeral, forms of writing—most sensitive to the demands of its age.

The essay uses prose, she tells them, again picking her metaphors with care, "to sting us wide awake and fix us in a trance which is not sleep but rather an intensification of life. The principle which controls it," you wonder? Simply this, she says, "that it should give pleasure. It should lay us under a spell with its first word, and we should only wake, refreshed, with its last."

"I agree that does sound tricky," says the woman with the dreadlocks, "but how is it more perilous than writing a novel?"

The essay, which by the way is the form of literature that "least calls for the use of long words," she offers, "admits more properly than biography or fiction of sudden boldness and metaphor." The danger, she advises, is that it "can be polished till every atom of its surface shines. Like the grapes on a Christmas-tree," she cautions, they might "glitter for a single night, but are dusty and garish the day after."

"What, then, makes a great essayist?"

Woolf stares out the window for a minute, her eyes narrowed in thought, before answering.

The greatest essays have a "wild flash of imagination, that lightning crack of genius in the middle which leaves them flawed and imperfect, but starred with poetry." There are moments, she says, in the best essays when the language soars from the page and takes the reader on its dazzling flight, full of beauty and music and brilliance. Moreover, the greatest essayists always successfully create that one essential element: a human voice, a true human voice. When you read a great essay, you feel the writer right there, almost in the room with you, her breath lingering on every page.

In other words, you'll find in the best essays that the "spirit of personality permeates every word." That, she exclaims with passion, "is the triumph of style."

And though nothing should appear more effortless than a well-written essay, she warns them, the work to achieve it is monumental. The writing of fine essays takes close and careful work. "The weighing of cadences, the consideration of pauses; the effect of repetitions and consonances and assonances—all this," she assures them, is "the duty of a writer who wishes to put a complex meaning fully and completely before his reader."

"You've written a lot of essays, haven't you?" the gray-haired woman asks.

Indeed, she has, she acknowledges. She published hundreds of essays and reviews for the *Times Literary Supplement* and the *Nation & Athenaeum* and even published a few in places like *Good*

Housekeeping, The New York Herald Tribune, The Yale Review, and *The Atlantic Monthly.* She took this writing of journalism very seriously. It steeped her in language, she explains, and it taught her to think more deeply about the art of reading as well as the art of writing. You see, she says, serious reading is essential to serious writing. Reading closely, taking detailed notes, she explains, allows you to weigh a book, to enjoy the writer's strengths and to understand his shortcomings. It was an important part of her creative enterprise, she reflects, this reading and measuring of others' work. And she enjoyed writing essays about the books she'd read; she liked meditating on the ways they had shaped her as a writer.

Reading, she proposes, thinking of the more practical souls in the class, can have quite a utilitarian value as well. There's nothing like reading someone else's words as a warm-up for writing.

" 'Read a little Shakespeare,' I'd jot in my diary, 'so as to loosen my muscles.' " Reading, I found, is a way to get ready to write because it prepares the mind to create. Perhaps, she speculates, that is because reading draws you away from the physical world and into the imagined one. Or because it stimulates the ear and the eye. Without a doubt, reading can spark, inspire, and nurture creativity because, she says with delight, it steeps us in imagination and makes us more aware of ourselves.

But then, one also reads for the sheer pleasure of it. For a long time, she tells them, she has harbored a great vision about readers.

"I have sometimes dreamt," she says, picking up a book,

"that when the Day of Judgment dawns and the great conquerors and lawyers and statesmen come to receive their rewards—their crowns, their laurels, their names carved indelibly upon imperishable marble—the Almighty will turn to Peter and will say, not without a certain envy when He sees us coming with our books under our arms, 'Look, these need no reward. We have nothing to give them here. They have loved reading.' "

She tucks the books under her arm and prepares to leave. Love reading, she reminds them before slipping from the room, and you will be better writers.

WRITING SPARKS

1. Write about the experience of reading a favorite book. Be careful to bring yourself into the action: How did you discover this particular book? Can you describe the cover, the binding, any illustrations? Are there any particular details of the day, the light, the time of year when you first read it that seem meaningful? Share with your reader something about your life at the time. Even if you can't quite pin it down, see if you can remember what the book meant to you and why. What did it rouse in your soul?

2. Telling the unflattering truths about oneself is,

Woolf argues, the hallmark of a good essayist. We admire the unflinching revelation, the candid admission. If you don't think you have the courage to put yourself out there, warts and all, in an essay, don't be afraid to try out the camouflage of fiction. Jot down some of your less desirable traits. Now use this list to develop a character for a story. Let yourself exaggerate the flaws for comic or dramatic effect. Use them to get your character into deeper and deeper trouble before you discover a way out.

3. Take a trip to the library or a bookstore. Your goal is to find a book you absolutely must read. You want something that will fascinate you, that will make you turn off the television. Any subject, any genre will do. The only requirement is that you choose according to your desire. As you read, record in your journal your emotional reaction to the book. When you've finished it, use your notes as inspiration for a short essay about reading.

4. Woolf begins "A Sketch of the Past" with her very first memory: sitting on her mother's lap looking at the red and purple flower pattern on her dress. Without trying to force a chronology, she lets this first memory lead freely to others. Begin an autobiographical essay by describing your very first memory. Don't be afraid to begin with just a fragment of memory. Observe it in close detail, then see what other memories emerge.

5. Experiment with reading as a warm-up for writing. Woolf sometimes liked to read a little Shakespeare to loosen up for writing, but select any author you like. Because their pieces tend to be short, anthologies often work well for this exercise. The only rule is to read something for ten minutes or so before you begin to write. If you find yourself resisting this exercise because it is a waste of time, discipline yourself to try it for just a week. After a week, determine if warming up for ten minutes made for more fruitful writing sessions.

6. Start your own memoir club with a group of friends. Begin by reading some memoirs: Woolf's *Moments of Being* is a good starting place. After you've gotten comfortable with the genre, members can begin writing their own short, essay-length memoirs. Remember, the beauty of the memoir is that it can focus on a brief period of time, even a single event. It need not offer a comprehensive view of your life, just a tantalizing morsel. Take turns at your meetings reading your memoirs to each other.

PUBLISHING

TOWARD THE END OF THE course, a serious-looking young man asks a question he has been hoarding for weeks.

"What advice do you have about getting published?"

A sigh slips involuntarily from Woolf's throat. The dreaded question. They are always so eager to publish, so hungry for it. They have no idea what bitter food it can be. Still, it must be dealt with. She squares her shoulders and readies herself for the onslaught.

"Publish nothing," she advises gravely, "before you are thirty."

She feels the entire room reel back in horror.

"But why?" a young man asks, his voice strained with a strong feeling of injustice.

"If you publish," she explains, "your freedom will be checked; you will be thinking what people will say; you will write for others when you ought only to be writing for yourself."

She knows, she tells them, what it is to be eager for recognition and validation. But give yourself the gift of apprenticeship.

Let yourself try and fail and try again without the pressure of publishing. Her own course, she admits, was perhaps extreme. She took nine years to write her first novel. She worked through five or six complete drafts of it, sometimes even starting entirely from scratch. Yes, it was long. Yes, it was arduous. But what she learned! How valuable to have those years to be a beginner.

"But you *did* publish it, right?" a woman asks earnestly.

She nods; yes, she did publish it. Eventually.

Looking at their bright faces, she decides not to tell them the entire truth. She doesn't tell them that the publication date of the novel had to be delayed for two years because she was so ill. She doesn't mention the months when she couldn't eat or write or think. They don't need to know how she would lie in bed listening to the voices of the dead, or how the doctors feared she would never recover her sanity. No, she decides, those days are too dark for this sunny, airy classroom.

So she explains instead how that first novel, *The Voyage Out*, was published by her half-brother's publishing firm just after her thirty-third birthday. The second novel came out four years later. But, she tells them, she was never really free to be herself, to write as she wished, until she and her husband began the Hogarth Press, their own publishing company. It wasn't until 1922 when they published her novel *Jacob's Room* that she began to feel truly free.

I felt at forty that I had finally "found out how to begin to say something in my own voice," she tells them, remembering the growing confidence threading through her.

A long time to be a beginner, she admits, yet she cannot help but believe that the years of practice helped prepare her for the novels that would follow, especially *Mrs. Dalloway* and *To the Lighthouse.* They were thrilling books to write, she tells them with excitement in her voice. She had been free to experiment, to tell a story in the way she wanted to tell it.

But, she warns, if you want to publish because you think it will make you famous and rich, then you must know that neither of those books brought her widespread fame. A highly regarded experimentalist she might have been considered at the time, but neither popular nor rich. As it turns out, it wasn't until that lark of a novel, that joke of a book, *Orlando* (her sixth novel, by the way, published at age forty-six, she reminds them) that she became a best-selling author.

Yes, she concedes, best-selling books do buy certain freedoms for writers. She has to say that she liked having enough money to turn down reviewing work she didn't want or to travel to France or to buy new clothes. But, she warns, best-selling books have their own kinds of traps. After the success of *Orlando,* she was pressured to produce a similar book.

At the time, I felt, "I could go on writing like that—the tug and suck are at me to do it." But, she tells her students, she didn't want merely to repeat her success. She wanted to strike out toward something new, something more poetic. What is the point of a new book, she asks, if it is not to solve a new problem? Of course it would have been easier emotionally and more lucrative financially to repeat her successes, but how would that have satisfied her creative vision?

She tells them she was extraordinarily lucky.

Because I could publish my own books, she boasts, I felt I was "the only woman in England free to write what I like."

"Is that why you started the Hogarth Press?" someone asks.

Honestly, she tells them, it was meant to be a hobby. She and her husband thought it would be relaxing to learn to set type, to learn to print. And they moved in talented artistic and literary circles, she explains, and enjoyed the idea of publishing the works of their friends. They wanted to publish books that commercial publishing wouldn't touch because they were too experimental or controversial. As it turned out, she says proudly, they published many wonderful writers: E. M. Forster, Rebecca West, Katherine Mansfield. They produced translations of Gorky, Tolstoy, Rilke, Dostoyevsky (whom she helped to translate, she adds), and, of course, Freud.

She had read the literary submissions. At first it was a treat to read the manuscripts; she liked writing encouraging letters to young writers. But, as the press grew from a hobby to a real business, she recalls, they became deluged with manuscripts, sometimes receiving more than six hundred a year. She can remember having a stack of manuscripts three feet thick on her desk. And not the kind of thing you dashed through either.

But it didn't quite begin that way. No, she laughs, it began with a secondhand press set up on the kitchen table. And what a mess! Ink and type everywhere. She and Leonard did everything: she set the type, Leonard printed the pages. But how they loved it. They were enthralled from the first. Did they know, she asks, that she had set the type herself for T. S. Eliot's great poem *The Waste Land*? You get to know a poem very well, she says gaily, when you set each letter yourself.

We published a great deal of new poetry at the press, she explains; it was one of the things, you could say, that distinguished us. And we were eager to publish the new generation of poets such as W. H. Auden, William Empson, and Stephen Spender, all of whom appeared in one of our publications called *New Signatures*. Later, some people called it a landmark. We had the good fortune to publish these up-and-coming poets early in their careers, and they ended up making a mark on the world of letters. It was our young partner, John Lehmann, we had to thank for that.

A soft-spoken young woman asks her if she ever wrote poetry.

Oh no! she cries. Well, except for one silly poem about a butcher, but no one needs to know about that, she smiles. For us prose writers poetry always seems a bit frightening.

"It must be like taking the veil and entering a religious order—observing the rites and rigours of metre," she jokes. "Could one say what one meant and observe the rules of poetry?"

She casts her eyes across the room scanning each face. She wonders if one could distinguish on sight the poets from the novelists. What is it, she wonders, that draws one to verse and the other to prose?

"So you don't like poetry?" someone says.

On the contrary, she assures them, what is more powerful, more beautiful than poetry? Some people even thought she was a poet, she admits. Some people called her a poet who wrote novels; they said she wrote a "poet's prose." Perhaps that is true, she reflects. I often aspired to infuse the power of poetry into my novels. There is no question of that.

Here is what I know about great poetry, she tells them. It "gives expression to sensation more vigorously, more exactly than we can manage for ourselves in the flesh. It is a world of astonishing physical brilliance and intensity; sharpened, intensified as objects are in a clearer air." It is so hard to explain, she thinks, this magic of poetry, how it transforms the world. We see things in poetry, she goes on, "such as we see them, not in dreams, but when all the faculties are alert and vigorous." We can even see ourselves more clearly, she contends, "under the more intense ray of poetry; under its sharper, its lovelier light."

"I've heard some say modern poetry is dead," the serious young woman asserts.

Yes, they have been saying that for some time; at least, I expect, since the Renaissance, she adds, trying to lighten the mood. The young woman repays her with a grim look, obliging Woolf to take a more serious tone.

She confesses she has what many would consider old-fashioned ideas about poetry. Take modern poets. They seem to have "all the virtues, and none of the gifts," she says, her voice taking on an air of irreverence. She hears a stifled gasp or two from around the room, but she doesn't stop. There is no question, she tells them, hers was a great age for lyric poetry.

But, she asserts, speaking directly to the poets in the room, "the lyric cry of ecstasy or despair, which is so intense, so personal, and so limited, is not enough. In poetry you get greater intensity than in prose, and have the right to be more jerky and disconnected. But I think you carry this right a little far. These are the chief criticisms I have to make; too much detail; too jerky; not sufficiently seen as a whole. On the other side; vividness; truthfulness, and often some striking observation."

She leans back in her chair. She can see that some of her students are not happy. They do not like what she has said of modern poetry. She reminds them that poetry has been used in the past to do so much more. All of Shakespeare's plays, she says standing up excitedly, were written in poetry.

My goodness, she cries waving her hand through the air, just think of all the things poetry used to do for us! Just remember all the roles you poets were happy to play! You wrote drama; you wrote comedy.

"You made us roar with laughter," she reminds them, "incredible though this now seems." She stops to let the thought sink in and then continues. "Later, you were lashing our follies, trouncing our hypocrisies, and dashing off the most brilliant of satires."

And now? she asks. Now you are shut up in a room by yourself. And what do you think about? Follies and hypocrisies? Laughter and satires? No. You think about yourself. She leans back against the chalkboard and sighs. "It is apparently easier to write a poem about oneself than about any other subject."

"Well," one student asks timidly, "what advice do you have for those of us who want to write poetry?"

Woolf notices how the sounds from the street drift into the

warm classroom. A bus trundles by, a throng of birds warbles in a nearby oak, the voices of pedestrians rise and fade as they pass. That is the source of poetry, Woolf thinks to herself, the world out there.

"Let your rhythmical sense wind itself in and out among men and women, omnibuses, sparrows—whatever comes along the street—until it has strung them together in one harmonious whole," she recommends. Absorb every experience that comes your way fearlessly. "Re-think human life into poetry and so give us tragedy again and comedy by means of characters." But characters, she adds, "not spun out at length in the novelist's way, but condensed and synthesised in the poet's way."

Don't you see, she says urgently, how inventing characters is essential to poetry? Essential to writing?

"So you are saying that inventing characters teaches us how to write poetry?" a man asks doubtfully.

Indeed it does, Woolf assures him.

"The art of having at one's beck and call every word in the language, of knowing their weights, colours, sounds, associations, and thus making them suggest more than they can state," she tells them excitedly, is learned most "effectively by imagining that one is not oneself but somebody different."

Why was Shakespeare such a genius? she asks. How did he learn what could be done with every syllable and sound in the English language? Because he imagined himself into characters of all kinds—lords and murderers, queens and commoners.

It was they who taught him to write, she says solemnly.

If you want to be poets, she advises them, "you will do well to embark upon a long poem in which people as unlike yourself as possible talk at the tops of their voices." She takes up her books, preparing to leave, then adds one last thought.

And for heaven's sake, she says, looking down and brushing some chalk dust from her skirt, "publish nothing before you are thirty." She raises her head to a sea of disappointed faces. Why don't they see, she wonders, that the joy must be in the poem, not in the publishing? The reward is in the writing, not in the approval of strangers. Then again, perhaps she has pressed this idea too far today. She remembers Keats and Shelley, neither of whom saw their thirtieth birthdays, and thinks perhaps it is time to relent just a little.

Of course, if it should so happen that you have written your best poems in your twenties, just remember, she adds in a gentle voice, "they wont spoil with the keeping."

Writing Sparks

1. If you have a publishing bug, begin to calm it by using your home computer or your local copy center to self-publish a "chapbook" of your best work. In the Renaissance, nicely printed books were extremely expensive, but small, cheap books were sold by peddlers known as "chapmen." Today, the word *chapbook* is used to mean a small, printed book of poetry, although

you can certainly commandeer it for short prose. Chapbooks are usually 8½-by-11-inch paper folded in half and are usually no more than twenty pages or so. For directions how to do this using MS Word, go to www.microsoft.com/Education/CreateBooklet. mspx.

2. For seven days in a row, sit in a public place (a coffee shop, a bus stop, a library, a city park) and take notes. Record everything, paying attention not just to sights, but to sounds and smells as well. Above all don't censor what at first doesn't seem "poetic." Include as many concrete details as you can. At the end of the week, write a long poem drawn from what you have observed. Include the odd, the ugly, or the ordinary, but make it part of a whole vision.

3. Woolf wrote jokingly to her friend Vita Sackville-West that she was tired of poets who did nothing but describe perfect buttercups. She demanded instead poems filled with facts, poems about the behavior of earthworms or the correct way to sanitize milk. Jot down some topics that primarily concern facts rather than emotions: for example, how to change a tire, the pollination habits of bees, or the process of bookbinding. Select one of them and research as many facts as you can. Use your research as the source of a longish (two- or three-page) poem. Allow yourself to be funny, serious, satirical, or earnest as the mood

strikes, but use compact language and strong images to transform facts into poetry.

4. Woolf believed that the intensity of poetry came from the poet's ability to select a few telling observations rather than overwhelming the reader with every detail. Poets, she wrote, "succeed by simplifying: practically everything is left out." Return to your poem of facts above, but revise it by picking two or three really suggestive details and leaving all the others out. The poem now should be less than a page.

5. Use the tools of the poet (striking imagery, concentrated language, metaphor, rhythm, even rhyme if you like) to tell a story. Use line breaks or write it as a "prose poem" without line breaks, but go for intensity, for language that becomes a kind of music. See the "Time Passes" section in *To the Lighthouse* for inspiration.

6. Every family has funny stories: the time your younger sister bought a pony on a TV auction or your brother laughed so hard milk came out of his nose. Take one of your comical family stories, but this time bring the episode to life in a poem. Immerse us in the atmosphere of the scene; let us feel the emotions of the moment. If you can, make us laugh out loud.

DOUBTING

Students shift nervously in their chairs as Woolf
sets her books down at the head of the long seminar table. It is
the last day of class. What has she forgotten, what has she left
out? she wonders. What must she say before they all go their
separate ways? Before she can even seat herself, a man blunders
out a question.

"But how do we know if we're really, I mean *really* novelists?
Is there any way to tell?"

Well, all real novelists, she says, lowering herself into
the smooth wooden chair, have a small birthmark just behind
their...She pauses and laughs. If it were only as easy as that.
How does one know?

"The novelist," she observes in a very quiet, serious voice,
"is terribly exposed to life. Taste, sound, movement, a few words
here, a gesture there, a man coming in, a woman going out, even
the motor that passes in the street or the beggar who shuffles
along the pavement, and all the reds and blues and lights and
shades of the scene claim his attention." Is this your sensibility?

she asks. Are you attuned to the world around you? Taking in this, noticing that?

A true novelist, she continues, shaping one of her sea images, "can no more cease to receive impressions than a fish in mid-ocean can cease to let the water rush through his gills." But collecting impressions is not enough, she warns them. The true art of the writer is to sift through the rush of impressions and cull out only the essential details.

"Life is forever pleading that she is the proper end of fiction," Woolf tells them blithely, forever trying to convince the novelist that "the more he sees of her and catches of her the better his book will be." Life does not add, Woolf says, shifting her voice in that tantalizing, secretive way, "that the side she flaunts uppermost is often, for the novelist, of no value whatever." Alone in his or her solitary room, Woolf tells them, the novelist must consider, must discriminate; must make life submit to art.

You see, she goes on, the writer cannot just pile up facts and descriptions. No. "The writer's task is to take one thing," she says very seriously, "and let it stand for twenty." She waits for a reaction. She notices the group has grown very quiet, very still.

She relieves their distress a little by admitting it is a difficult and dangerous task, this selecting of the essential detail from one's myriad of impressions, but this is the work of the novelist.

"Each sentence must have," she encourages, "at its heart, a little spark of fire. And this, whatever the risk, the novelist must pluck with his own hands from the blaze."

"But whenever I even think about beginning," an earnest brown-eyed man explains, "it all seems so overwhelming. For one thing, I am never sure where I am going. Shouldn't I know where I am going before I start?"

How can you possibly know, Woolf thinks to herself.

"The main thing in beginning a novel is to feel, not that you can write it," she says, "but that it exists on the far side of a gulf, which words can't cross: that its to be pulled through only in a breathless anguish." She knows what she has to say will sound strange, but she must say it. "A novel, to be good, should seem, before one writes it, something unwriteable." Of course, she tells them, this is just her way. If a novel seemed easy to do, she would have felt it not worth doing.

And you must be committed with all your writing, she counsels, to revise—revise diligently, revise steadily. It was not unusual for her to revise six or seven times, she confesses. You must read your work and weigh each word. Listen to the rhythm of your sentences. She laughs to herself when she remembers how she would read her lines aloud while taking her morning bath. Her housekeeper, she remembers, found the technique a bit alarming. Nevertheless, she tells them, whether you are writing verse or writing prose, you must test your words against your ear. When their music carries you effortlessly forward, as if you were the merest leaf on the crest of a wave, then you have found your sentence.

"But what makes an entire novel good? Is it just beautiful sentences stitched one to the next?" a soft-spoken woman asks.

A wonderful question, Woolf thinks to herself. And just

think of the multitude of answers that have been offered in reply. Her students watch her with such eagerness, she realizes that they probably imagine this is the most difficult question of the course, when to her mind, it is, perhaps, the easiest.

"One element," she says concentrating her words, "remains constant in all novels." The class leans forward eager to get the nugget they've been waiting for all these weeks. "And that," she says with confidence, "is the human element."

Novels, she reminds them, are about people. They thrill us, she explains, because "they excite in us the feelings that people excite in us in real life." She tilts her head to the side, detecting an air of dissatisfaction. A woman in a colorful scarf speaks up.

"Novels all seem so different," she says. "Are you saying that they're all just about character? That's it? That seems kind of limiting."

Oh dear, Woolf thinks, they have not yet reflected enough on the art of fiction. Just consider the astonishing number of ways to explore character already invented, she tells them, let alone the ways yet to be created. She decides she must make it plain, so she asks them to imagine a character. This character is an old woman, she says. We shall call her Mrs. Brown. Let's think of all the ways one might reveal Mrs. Brown.

Now, an English writer of my day, she says, "would bring out her oddities and mannerisms; her buttons and wrinkles; her ribbons and warts. Her personality would dominate the book. A French writer would rub out all that; he would sacrifice the individual Mrs. Brown to give a more general view of human nature; to make a more abstract, proportioned, and harmonious whole. The Russian would pierce through the flesh; would reveal the soul—the soul alone, wandering out into the Waterloo Road, asking of life some tremendous question which would sound on and on in our ears after the book was finished."

She settles back a moment and watches them. She sees their questions mustering under the surface.

"And do you think dialogue is the best way to create character?" someone asks.

"Be chary of dialogue," Woolf warns, as it "puts the most violent pressure upon the reader's attention." Just think, she tells them, when you use dialogue, it's your reader who must figure out what the tone should sound like or what unspoken thoughts weave their way through the words the character speaks. No, she's always been circumspect about dialogue. A tool to use sparingly, she advises.

Whenever you give your characters words to speak, she tells them solemnly, it must be because what they have to say is so crucial to the story that it cannot be left out. If it is not of central importance, resist the temptation to include it.

But how she hates spouting things that sound like rules. She doesn't want to tell them what to do or think. She wants them to consider the tools they have at hand, but not to dictate how they use them. She wants to encourage them to create their own tools if they can. Each generation of writers must, she tells them, find their own way.

The job of all writers, she goes on, is "to preserve more sincerely and exactly what interests and moves them, even if to do so they must discard most of the conventions which are commonly observed by the novelist." Remember, the novel, even now, is still young, still fertile. "We are aware of relations and subtleties which have not yet been explored." That is because it is a living, growing thing. Don't we still feel that there is something that has not yet been said? Prose, she tells them, is still so youthful that "we scarcely know what powers it may not hold concealed within it." She watches their faces as they absorb this daunting thought. But she wants to offer one more piece of advice.

And, she adds, "I am by no means confining you to fiction. Write books of travel and adventure, and research and scholarship, and history and biography, and criticism and philosophy and science. Write all kinds of books, hesitating at no subject however trivial or however vast."

Then a woman who has not spoken a word the entire term poses the question that every person in the room secretly harbors in his or her heart. "What," she says quietly, "if we're not good enough?" The room grows unearthly quiet, as if every breath were hanging suspended in the warm afternoon light.

How often, Woolf thinks, has she asked herself just that question? How often has she doubted whether she had achieved anything? "Is it nonsense?" she has wondered, or "is it brilliance?" Yet in the end, does it matter? She wants to find a way to tell them what it has all meant to her, this writing life.

"The greatest rapture known to me," she confides, has been writing. I have been happiest when I have been imagining scenes and inventing characters; the world has been a delight when I have been composing, all of my being immersed, focused, complete. Being a writer, she wants them to understand, being someone who observes the world with intensity and records it with care, gives them the chance to live a rich life, whether they ever become successful writers or not.

Suddenly, a worn copy of *To the Lighthouse* perched on top of a spiral notebook catches her eye. Taking up the book she looks at its worn cover, her sister's imagistic lighthouse still standing very upright, throwing its spray of light into the sky.

As I think I have said to you before, she begins very slowly, "I prefer, where truth is important, to write fiction."

Opening the book to the last page, she begins to read aloud in that low, melodious, magical voice.

"There it was—her picture. Yes, with all its greens and blues, its lines running up and across, its attempt at something. It would be hung in the attics, she thought; it would be destroyed. But what did that matter? she asked herself, taking up her brush again. She looked at the steps; they were empty; she looked at her canvas; it was blurred."

Woolf pauses, as if experiencing again herself the hesitation, the blurriness, the excitement. She continues, her voice vibrating. "With a sudden intensity, as if she saw it clear for a second, she drew a line there, in the centre. It was done; it was finished. Yes, she thought, laying down her brush in extreme fatigue, I have had my vision."

She stops. She sets down the book. She looks at the class, her face flushed with pleasure.

I have had my vision, her look seems to say to them; now you must go and have yours.

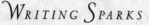

WRITING SPARKS

1. Whether you are often in airports, classrooms, offices, highways, or playgrounds, you can train yourself to observe character. Create a special section of your journal devoted to collecting observations about people you come across in your daily life. Note gestures, word patterns, clothes, gaits, expressions, and so on. Challenge yourself to collect ten character observations a week.

2. It can be useful to compare the strengths of different tools for creating character. For this exercise, focus on two characters in conflict—a couple disagreeing over what kind of dog to buy at the pet store, a parent and teen in conflict over curfew, girlfriends who like the same guy having different ideas about what to do about it—and write a simple description of the scene. Describe looks, gestures, thoughts, but use no dialogue. You can describe what the characters say—for example, he told her to be quiet—but do not give the characters' actual words. For the next part of the exercise, write the same scene using *only* dialogue. The scene should only be conversation, no description at all. Now compare the two scenes and determine the power of each tool. (This is a fun

exercise to do with a writing group.) Last, select the essential description and the essential dialogue from each of your drafts and combine them to render the characters and the scene fully.

3. Think back to a conflict between two people you've either observed or been a part of. The conflict can be over anything. Perhaps it concerns a man and a woman arguing about who should pay for dinner, or a bus driver trying to get an unruly rider to comply with company policy, siblings fighting over the remote control, or even grandmothers picking the best name for their new granddaughter. Try to remember as many details about the scene as you can. Do you remember the clothes, the gestures, or the words hurled at each other? Write the scene being careful to convey just the details that make the reader feel as if she's right there in the middle of it.

4. Use Woolf's descriptions of English, French, and Russian writers to explore three ways to develop character. Try writing three descriptions of Mrs. Brown—or any other character you'd like to use— using the elements of the three national styles Woolf describes. The English description of Mrs. Brown would focus on her appearance and her idiosyncrasies. It should emphasize her individuality in terms of her looks and behavior. Give us a keen sense of her beliefs and her quirks. The French style lets us see her as a person of a certain class or kind.

Nannies, for instance, always wear a particular kind of coat and hat, read a particular sort of book, and have a prescribed set of views about the disciplining of children. The description would be very spare and the last line of the description would reveal a deep insight into this sort of person. Last, according to Woolf, the Russian would dig deep into Mrs. Brown's core and show us her very soul. The description would show the character struggling with some fundamental question of human existence. We know the character because we know the internal struggle that shapes her every move.

5. Woolf loved to experiment with form and encouraged younger writers to do so. Writing to her nephew who was an aspiring writer, she suggested that he invent a new medium that was part poetry, part fiction, and part drama. Just for the fun of it, try your own experiments with form. Write something that is part poetry and part novel. But don't restrict yourself. Depending on your interests, you could try combining music, dance, sculpture, hypertext, images, podcasts, or anything else that appeals to you. It doesn't matter whether you succeed in inventing a new form, only that you have attempted to say something meaningful about your time, your place, or your life using the mediums that make sense to you.

SUGGESTED FURTHER READING

A GREAT DEAL HAS BEEN written about Virginia Woolf's life and work. Indeed, there is so much material that the real question is where to begin.

For a delicious sampler of Woolf's work, pick up *The Virginia Woolf Reader*. In this handy single volume, editor Mitchell Leaska offers illustrative excerpts from Woolf's major novels, short stories, essays, diaries, and letters. From there, you will very likely want to read some of Woolf's novels in full. I recommend beginning with *Mrs. Dalloway* or *To the Lighthouse;* both novels create rich portraits of English social life in the first part of the twentieth century. For a taste of Woolf's comedy, try *Orlando,* a novel about a young Renaissance nobleman who lives for three hundred years and magically transforms into a woman. Dog lovers should also pick up *Flush,* a portrait of the great English poet Elizabeth Barrett Browning from the point of view of her cocker spaniel.

To get a sense of Woolf's powerful nonfiction prose style, read *A Room of One's Own.* In this witty, playful essay, Woolf defends her notion that women need five hundred pounds a year and a room of their own if they are to write fiction. Many of her other important essays about women and creativity— including the essential "Professions for Women"—have been collected by Michele Barrett in *Women and Writing*, a book well worth exploring.

A Writer's Diary: Being Extracts from the Diary of Virginia Woolf, edited by Woolf's husband, Leonard Woolf, contains a beautiful selection of excerpts that focus largely on Woolf's creative life. Its revealing portrait may inspire you to read all five volumes of her complete diary. *Congenial Spirits: The Selected Letters of Virginia Woolf*, edited by Joan Trautmann Banks, offers a sampling of Woolf's lively correspondence.

Two books collect memories from those who knew Woolf personally and create their own compelling portraits. *Recollections of Virginia Woolf*, edited by Joan Russell Noble, includes entries from several members of the Bloomsbury group, people who worked with the Woolfs, and a variety of writers including Rebecca West, T. S. Eliot, and E. M. Forster. *Virginia Woolf: Interviews and Recollections* covers some of the same territory, but also includes contributions from additional writers and friends including one from a woman who was a student at Girton College and was present the night Woolf gave the talk that would eventually become *A Room of One's Own*. The recently published *Afterwords: Letters on the Death of Virginia Woolf*, by Sybil Oldfield, collects more than two hundred condolence letters sent to Woolf's husband and sister after her death. The range of people who wrote—from dignitaries to common readers—and the outpouring of emotion they express creates a powerful testament to Woolf's life and work.

There have been a number of important biographies of Woolf produced over the years, but several are particularly outstanding. First is *Virginia Woolf: A Biography,* written by her nephew Quentin Bell. Family bias aside, one must acknowledge something singular about a biography written by someone who knew his subject personally. Lyndall Gordon's *A Writer's Life* offers indispensable insight into Woolf's creativity and her creative life. Teachers and those looking for a more brief account of Woolf's life should see Ruth Webb's *Virginia Woolf,* part of the British Library writers series. Its wonderful maps, photographs, and facsimiles of letters and manuscripts are a feast for the eyes. Finally, Hermione Lee's *Virginia Woolf* is brilliant, balanced, and supremely readable.

SPARKS

~~~~~~~

VIRGINIA WOOLF BELIEVED THAT WE could teach ourselves to be writers. Writing, she argued, need not be the pro-
vince of a handful of well-educated men. Ordinary people,
those she liked to call "commoners and outsiders," could train
themselves. By writing daily and reading extensively, she argued,
"we teach ourselves how to read and to write, how to preserve,
and how to create."

The following pages provide a variety of exercises that allow
writers to work on their skills just as Woolf did in her diaries
and notebooks. Some are very gentle warm-ups, serving as
preparation for writing: taking a walk, for example, or keeping
lists of ideas and observations. Others provide opportunities
for stylistic exploration, for example, learning how simple
changes in syntax or diction can create very different effects.
The fiction exercises that follow focus on elements such as dialogue, narration, and character development. The nonfiction
exercises explore ideas for writing essays, biographies, and
memoirs. Finally, the poetry prompts are based on Woolf's

idiosyncratic but interesting advice for poets. Each of the exercises has been drawn from Woolf's own writing, from her novels, essays, and memoirs. A number of them point you to places in her work that can serve as models for your own experiments.

Remember that these exercises are not recipes for stories or poems. Don't expect that doing them will lead to a completed work. Rather, think of them more as informal afternoons in the kitchen where you work on cracking eggs without getting any shell into the batter or learning how to knead bread so that it will rise. The exercises help you build the skills you need to make your creation, but they are not the creation itself. That must come through the mystery of the creative process that combines ideas, passion, and skill into a work of art.

The ease or difficulty of any given exercise will depend on each writer's experience and sensibility. What will seem basic for one writer will seem adventurous to another. For that reason, there is no prescribed order for doing them. Some writers will focus on a particular genre; others may want to range freely, doing whatever exercises strike their fancy. Just as there is no designated order, there is also no right way of doing any particular exercise. Some writers will follow them to the letter; others will adapt them; still others, I imagine, might strike out in an entirely new direction altogether. Any or all of these methods would be appropriate.

That said, it would be a mistake to work only on the exercises that come easily. Woolf stretched herself as far as she could with every new book, taking risks, trying experiments she wasn't sure she could accomplish. Follow her example and push yourself to discover, or at least glimpse, the far reaches of your own creativity.

A few words for teachers using this book. I have found that asking students to share the results of their exercises with each other lets them see how writers solve creative challenges in excitingly different ways. They often amaze themselves and each other with the wildly different and interesting solutions they discover. Using some of the collaborative exercises I've included here not only adds an element of surprise to the writing, but also helps create a stronger sense of community where students feel safe to experiment and share their work.

BEGINNINGS

Sometimes stories would come to Woolf in a bolt of inspiration, but her regular sources of ideas came from daily reading and writing. Always open to creative ideas, she made a habit of jotting them down in her diary or on any handy scrap of paper. According to her housekeeper, she left little piles of paper all around the house—on tabletops, the seats of chairs, heaped on the mantel—anywhere an interesting idea struck her. If you aren't quite ready to clutter your house with scrap paper, then try out some of the following exercises to jump-start your own creative process. The ideas you'll find here include building a writing community, getting into the habit of collecting ideas for writing, and discovering ways to create inventive opening lines for your stories.

I. Woolf, her siblings, and Bloomsbury friends liked to get together regularly to talk about ideas and share their work. For "Thursday Evenings," they gathered to talk about art and politics. For the "Novel Club," which later turned into the "Memoir Club," they would read works in progress. They also had a play-reading club for a while. Take the Bloomsbury lead and gather fellow writers to share ideas and work. Create a club or group that meets at least once every month; coffee shops and cafés make good meeting spots.

2. Start keeping a reading journal to generate creative ideas. "To begin reading with a pen in my hand," Woolf recorded in her diary, "discovering, pouncing, thinking of phrases, when the ground is new, remains one of my great excitements." As you read, jot down phrases or descriptions that you find powerful. Notice various techniques. For example, how does a particular writer develop character? Is there a great deal of external description or do we see more of the character's thoughts? Once you train yourself to notice how other writers use language, you can begin to try out some of their techniques for yourself. See *A Writer's Diary* for inspiration.

3. Surrender the notion that you must know everything about a story before you can write it. Remember, for many months Woolf used the working title *The Hours* for the novel that would become *Mrs. Dalloway*. Even more striking, the character of Septimus Warren Smith, one of the central characters of that book, was a late addition. "One must begin by being chaotic," Woolf wrote in her diary. Post this quotation in your writing area, then give

yourself permission to begin, even if you don't know where you are going. Remember: uncertainty is an essential part of creativity.

4. Woolf's instinct for beginnings often started with a character in the middle of an action: Betty Flanders fitfully writes a letter in *Jacob's Room;* Clarissa Dalloway leaves to buy flowers for her party; Mrs. Ramsay assures her son that they will go to the lighthouse. Make a list of ten beginnings that place a character squarely in the middle of an action that has some significance. (Don't worry if you don't know much about your character yet; let yourself take a leap.) Pick the most promising of your openings and use it as the beginning of a new story. (In a writing group, share opening lines with each other. Give away an opening line for someone else's story.)

5. Sometimes Woolf opens her novels with an answer to an unspoken question. For example, in *To the Lighthouse* James has asked whether they will be sailing to the lighthouse the next day; in *Mrs. Dalloway,* a servant has asked if she should get the flowers for the party. Think about ways opening with questions can jump-start your story. Here are some examples of opening questions that immediately suggest action.

  a. "How many fingers am I holding up?"
  b. "Where is this bus headed?"

c. "Who was the woman I saw you with yes-
terday?"

d. "Is that really a word?"

Either make up your own question or use one of
the above to begin a story.

STRUCTURE

Woolf felt she had no talent for creating plots. "I can make up
situations," she acknowledged, "but I cannot make up plots."
Nevertheless, her stories always possess an organizing principle
and the essential elements of structure: a beginning, middle,
and end.

When conceiving *To the Lighthouse,* Woolf drew a picture in
her notebook to describe the structure: "two blocks joined by a
corridor." For *Mrs. Dalloway,* time became an organizing principle. She confines the story to a single day and uses the chiming
of clocks to register the faint, but persistent passing of time.

1. Experiment with time as a structuring principle by
limiting your story to a single day. Begin in the morning with two characters in conflict. By midday, com-
plicate the conflict. By night, settle or complete the
conflict one way or another.

2. If you are inspired by visual forms, you might create
a geometric story structure as Woolf did with *To the*

Lighthouse. The two blocks in her scheme represented two time periods and the connecting corridor was the ten-year stretch between them. Can you imagine a geometric shape for a story you have in mind? Points of a triangle meeting in the middle? Concentric circles? Or use Woolf's own scheme to create a structure for your own story.

SCENE

Whenever Woolf passed a person or observed an incident that captured her interest, she felt she would "without knowing I do it, instantly make up a scene." Scene building, she felt, was the essence of her creative gift.

A good scene in fiction lets the reader see the action and watch the characters interact. Typically, it occurs in one place and at one time. For example, the famous dinner scene in *To the Lighthouse* ("The Window," section XVII) makes us feel that we are sitting with the Ramsays in their dining room, hearing their conversation, smelling their food, and seeing the candlelight shimmer in the windows. We grow uncomfortable when one guest orders more soup and two others arrive late, waiting to see what Mr. and Mrs. Ramsay's reactions will be. When dinner is over and the guests disperse, the scene ends.

The dinner scene is effective because it dramatizes the action, it shows us the events unfolding before our very eyes. In this way, it creates a sense of both immediacy and suspense:

what is going to happen? Most important, scene building—dramatizing your characters' situation—is one of the best ways to follow that primary writing rule: show, don't tell.

1. Write a story about an item being lost and found, but limit yourself to three scenes. The first scene should dramatize the moment the item was discovered to be missing. The second scene should show the anguish about or complications from the loss. The final scene should show the object being returned or recovered or relinquished forever. Use setting, description, dialogue, action, gestures, and thoughts to make your reader feel that he or she is watching the events as they unfold.

2. Although scenes should have a kind of immediacy, the ways one might render a scene are myriad. Woolf deeply admired the Russian writers of her time, especially Turgenev and Dostoyevsky. She felt that Turgenev revised his scenes until they included only those elements that were indispensable. According to Woolf, he "states the essential and lets the reader do the rest." By contrast, she felt Dostoyevsky thought everything mattered and supplied his "reader with every possible help and suggestion." Write two versions of the same scene. In the first, put in every detail you can imagine to bring the scene before the reader's eyes. In the second, omit everything but the very essence. For example,

where you had a character using many gestures in the first, give him only one in the second; where you described all of a character's features in the first, describe only the one defining feature in the second; where the characters spoke dozens of lines of dialogue in the first, trim it to a handful of exchanges in the second.

CONFLICT

Conflict is the engine of a story: it puts characters in motion and keeps them going. Woolf's work includes internal conflicts—Cam Ramsay feeling torn between her loyalty to her brother and her love for her father—as well as external conflicts—Septimus Warren Smith trying to escape from being committed to a mental asylum.

Conflict builds momentum by increasing or getting more complicated. At the beginning of *To the Lighthouse,* for example, James is angry with his father for saying they won't be going to the lighthouse the next day. The conflict develops when his parents argue and James's hatred for his father grows. We continue to see the conflict—and its consequences—on the trip ten years later. Mr. Ramsay's praise of James resolves it—at least temporarily. In *Mrs. Dalloway,* Septimus Warren Smith resists Dr. Bradshaw's diagnosis; he does not want to be taken away to a home. Hearing someone come up the stairs escalates the conflict for Septimus, making him feel that he must take matters into his own hands. The consequence of this conflict is one of the great tragedies of the novel.

Harnessing the energy of conflict can be one of the most difficult challenges for beginning fiction writers. The following exercises will give you a chance to practice thinking about conflict and putting it to use in your own stories.

1. Our lives are surrounded by conflicts large and small. Start looking around and keeping a list of the conflicts you see: find them in your own life, your friends' lives, or just invent them. Include everything from the absurd to the sublime. For example, a person likes to sleep with the window open, but his partner doesn't; a woman's dog is constantly chewing up her shoes; a next-door neighbor plays music too loud; a man loses his job because someone starts a vicious rumor about him; a woman is about to be appointed to a position of authority she doesn't want; someone has to save a school full of children during a dangerous hurricane. As your list grows, note the ways that the conflicts might get worse before they get better.

2. Take an item from your conflict list and use it in a short story. Be sure to escalate the conflict at least two or three times before resolving it—happily, sadly, or ambiguously—at the end. If you are having trouble understanding conflict, you can also think about it in terms of your character's desires

and the things that happen that prevent him or her from realizing those desires. For example, Septimus wants to be a free man. Dr. Bradshaw's diagnosis puts that desire in jeopardy. Hearing someone coming up the stairs to take him away appears to Septimus to be the moment when he will lose his freedom entirely.

3. Character and conflict are inextricably connected. To see this principle in action, put different characters in the same situation and see what they do.

   a. A father tells his child the trip to the lighthouse won't happen. Pick two of the following characters and write a scene for each, showing how their reactions would differ:

     1) a little boy who dreams of going to the lighthouse

     2) a little girl who is afraid of boats

     3) a teenage girl who'd rather stay with her boyfriend

     4) a teenage boy who hates his father

   b. A woman tells a man she does not want to marry him. The men might include an elderly botanist, an insecure student, an opium-smoking poet, or a handsome young man. Write two sketches using the same conflict, the same woman, but different men in each.

4. Write a scene involving two friends who have dramatically conflicting desires. Show us the conflict, but do not let your characters discuss it openly. Look at the scene in *Mrs. Dalloway* where Elizabeth and Miss Kilman have tea for an example of one way to present this.

CHARACTER

Woolf's novels are powerful because of the complex, deeply human characters she creates. The techniques she uses to create her rich characters include:

Interior Thoughts: Woolf reveals her characters' rich inner lives; we know their thoughts, memories, fears, and loves. "How I dig out beautiful caves behind my characters," she wrote in her diary. "I think that gives exactly what I want; humanity, humour, depth." For example, as Mrs. Ramsay says the weather will be fine for the trip to the lighthouse, we are immediately thrust into the rapid stream of her interior thoughts. We find that she is worried about finishing the stocking she is knitting so it can be taken to the lighthouse the next day, which leads her to imagine the feelings of the keeper and his son and the narrow range of their lives; this current of thought builds until she convinces herself they must be terrified of a storm coming and sweeping them away. This idea then eddies back to the present with Mrs. Ramsay telling her daughters they must do what they can for the lighthouse keeper.

Others' Descriptions: Usually the only way we know what a character looks like in Woolf's novels is because another character comments on it. For example, we know that Mrs. Ramsay is "very clearly Greek, straight, blue-eyed" because that is how her friend William Bankes sees her. We know about Lily Briscoe's "Chinese eyes," because that is how Mrs. Ramsay describes her.

Actions: What a character does sometimes tells us more than what a character says. For example, in *Mrs. Dalloway* Sally Seton pawns a brooch in order to visit a country house, runs naked from the bathroom, and then kisses Clarissa in the garden. From these actions, the reader realizes that she is a free spirit who doesn't really care about conforming to social expectations. The fact that she later marries a wealthy man and has five children adds a layer of complication to her character.

Living Spaces: What a character's room looks like can also tell us a great deal about him or her. In *Jacob's Room*, we see Jacob's university room filled with photographs, a pipe, a Greek dictionary with poppies pressed between the pages, and a pair of very shabby slippers. The Ramsays' beach house in *To the Lighthouse* is a ramshackle mess: the wallpaper is peeling; there are sand, seaweed, and shells everywhere.

Others' Thoughts: What others say or think about someone helps to add dimension and depth to his or her character. For example, before the war, Septimus's employer not only thought him a man of excellent ability, but expected him to reach a very high position in the company. William Bankes remembers Mr. Ramsay pointing out a mother hen protecting her chicks. Bankes believes this shows Ramsay's "sympathy with humble things." Significantly, this is something Ramsay's children don't understand about their father, and it adds an important dimension to this complex man.

1. Write a sketch about a mother and daughter or father and son doing something together. Emphasize the characters' inner thoughts during their interaction to show us who these people are and what their relationship with each other is like.

2. Instead of letting an omniscient narrator provide an objective description of your characters, write a story in which we know about someone's physical appearance only because of another character's observations.

3. Using a work in progress, add another character's observations or memories to create a new dimension to what we know of a main character's personality, values, or background.

4. Practice developing character by making a list of attributes; for example: carefree, spontaneous, uptight,

miserly, independent, thoughtful, mean. For each attribute, provide three actions that demonstrate it. For example, a miserly character would not leave a tip, would set the thermostat at fifty-two degrees all winter, and would wear the same suit every day. This is a good exercise for practicing the "show, don't tell" principle.

5. Write a sketch involving two characters. Each character should have one of the attributes from the list above. Don't tell us what the attributes are; let the actions reveal them.

6. One thing that makes characters complex, and more real, is their contradictions. Write a sketch in which a character's words are at odds with his or her actions.

7. Woolf was frustrated when writing an early draft of *Mrs. Dalloway* because she thought her main character, Clarissa Dalloway, was somehow "tinselly." To solve this problem, she created memories for Clarissa that provided the depth and dimension she had felt was lacking. Return to a story in progress whose main character seems emotionally thin or one-dimensional and invent memories for him or her. Because the memories will add complexity to your character, expect to make other changes. Once you begin to understand more about this character, you may discover that he or she will do things or act in ways you might not have realized before.

8. In a sketch or a work in progress, describe a character's home or office to reveal an unexpected element of his or her personality. Characters become more interesting when we see that they have quirky, unexpected qualities, so don't be afraid to let us learn something that might take us by surprise.

9. Let a famous writer make an appearance in one of your stories. Create a comic effect by making your portrait highly irreverent. See Woolf's portrait of Shakespeare as a shabby barfly in *Orlando* for inspiration.

10. Write a sketch of a character who sees visions of the dead. Keep in mind that the seer need not be mad and the dead need not be scary, although this is the case for Woolf's Septimus Warren Smith.

11. Write a sketch in which your character's main conflict arises from her secret dream to live a different life.

12. A character's actions toward laborers, employees, or clerks can speak volumes about his or her personality. Show your character interacting with a clerk, flight attendant, employee, and so on, as a way to reveal something significant about him or her. Think about Clarissa Dalloway's interaction with the flower shop clerk as an example.

13. Write a story in which your main character mysteriously changes from a man to a woman (or vice versa) in the middle of the story. The focus shouldn't be

on the change, but on how the character's life has been transformed in unpredictable ways. See *Orlando* for hilarious inspiration.

14. Write a sketch of two characters meeting for the first time. Include their inner thoughts and let us see how they read each other's appearance, body language, conversation style, and what assumptions they draw about the other.

15. Using a work in progress, give one of the main characters added dimension by revealing what book (or other reading material) he or she carries around or what recurring dream he or she has.

16. Ambivalence, or being "made to feel violently two opposite things at the same time" as Woolf's Lily Briscoe says, is a powerful and difficult emotion. Write a sketch putting your character in a situation where he or she is torn in two directions.

17. Although we don't know minor characters as well as central characters, remind yourself to allow them some complexity, too. In a work in progress, use one or two of the character development techniques described here to enhance a minor character. Look at Charles Tansley or Miss Kilman for examples of fascinatingly complex minor characters.

POINT OF VIEW AND NARRATION

Woolf loved playing with point of view. Just think of *To the Lighthouse:* although it appears to use a third-person narrator (using *he* and *she* to describe the characters and the action), in fact we spend most of the novel moving among the interior thoughts of the various characters.

In some of her short works, Woolf uses first-person narrators whose limited views restrict our view of the world. For example, in "The Mark on the Wall" the narrator tries to figure out how the wall in her room has become stained. The story follows the narrator's thoughts—which invariably take a variety of tangents—as she tries to identify the stain. Not until the end of the story do we discover that it is not a stain at all, but a snail.

Woolf also played with intrusive narrators who comment on their own roles as storytellers. She has great fun with this technique in *Orlando,* where the biographer-narrator can't seem to keep track of his subject and shies away from the story whenever he suspects anything faintly immoral going on.

I. Write a sketch using a first-person narrator who misreads a situation because he or she has either misunderstood an essential element, has been deliberately misled about it, or is simply lacking a key piece of information. Let the narrator discover the truth only in the last sentence. See "The Mark on the Wall" for an example.

2. Woolf created a priggish biographer to narrate her comic novel *Orlando*. Constantly troubled by the difficulty of telling Orlando's life truthfully—especially once he mysteriously transforms into a woman—the narrator is constantly turning to the reader to explain why he can't really say what happened at this point in her life, or to describe why the art of biography is so difficult. To get a feel for the possibilities of an intrusive narrator, write a sketch using a narrator who is also continually commenting on his inability to tell his story. If you like, let your narrator speak directly to the reader explaining why this particular story is so difficult to tell. Remember that this technique is especially useful in creating comic effects.

3. One way to experiment with a third-person narrator who reveals the interior thoughts of a variety of characters is to begin with a simple dialogue sequence. For example, if we stripped the first few pages of *To the Lighthouse* of all the interior thoughts of the characters and left only the dialogue they exchange, it would read something like:

"Yes, of course, if it's fine tomorrow. But you'll have to be up with the lark," says Mrs. Ramsay.

"But, it won't be fine," says Mr. Ramsay.

"But it may be fine—I expect it will be fine," repeats Mrs. Ramsay, knitting impatiently.

"It's due west," says Charles Tansley, holding his

bony fingers spread so that the wind blows through them.

"Nonsense," says Mrs. Ramsay.

"There'll be no landing at the Lighthouse tomorrow," Tansley repeats, clapping his hands together. "No going to the Lighthouse, James."

"Perhaps you will wake up and find the sun shining and the birds singing," counters Mrs. Ramsay as she smooths the boy's hair. "Perhaps it will be fine tomorrow."

What "happens" in the scene occurs, of course, between the lines of dialogue. There Woolf explores each character's thoughts, memories, feelings, and ideas. Experiment with this kind of "writing between the lines." Write a dialogue between two characters having a disagreement, being sure to give each character three to five lines to speak. Once you have the dialogue, write one or two paragraphs between every line of the conversation showing what each character is thinking, feeling, and remembering as he or she talks.

4. Write a sketch of an unhappy person. First show her from the point of view of someone who doesn't like her. Then let us see her from the inside. Look at characters such as Charles Tansley from *To the Lighthouse* or Miss Kilman from *Mrs. Dalloway* for inspiration.

5. If you are writing about a social group (a family, a school clique, a team), try incorporating the point of view of an outsider to reveal qualities about the group that they cannot recognize about themselves.

6. To write from other people's points of view, you must be able to get under their skins. You must be able to think of the kind of words they would use, the sort of preoccupations they would have, the sort of memories that would be vivid to them. To practice this, write a sketch from the point of view of a person much younger than you, much older than you, or of the opposite sex.

SETTING

Woolf's settings imprint themselves on her characters. For Clarissa Dalloway, London is an exhilarating dazzle of activity that feels part of her lifeblood. The rhythm of the sea and the regular strokes of the lighthouse provide a kind of cadence for Mrs. Ramsay's thoughts. Woolf doesn't just create vivid descriptions of place, but reveals how these places shape the minds and temperaments of her characters.

1. Create a sketch about two characters who live in your hometown. One of them loves the town, the other hates it. Let each character walk to a coffee shop where they have planned to meet. Give each

one a different route, but base their paths on actual
streets in your town. Alternate between each character and provide their thoughts as they approach
their destination. Involve us not only in your characters but in the atmosphere of your hometown.
Look at Clarissa Dalloway's walk through London
for ideas.

DIALOGUE

What is most striking about Woolf's novels is how little the
things people say reflect the depth and intensity of what they
are thinking and feeling. In fact, many of her characters have
difficulty expressing what they really think and feel.

Nevertheless, Woolf uses dialogue—albeit sparingly—to
develop conflict and to reveal character. For example, when
Mrs. Ramsay and Tansley differ on the matter of the trip to
the lighthouse, their dialogue shows not just their different
ideas about the weather but also their disparate attitudes
toward life. Similarly, Mr. Ramsay's spasmodic outbursts, especially the line "We perish, each alone," reveals his self-absorbed
despair.

I. Read the dialogue from a work in progress aloud.
How does it sound in the open air? Have you given
your characters words that sound like real people
talking to each other? If you notice that you tend to

be wordy, challenge yourself to cut your dialogue in half. Go through each line and cut as close to 50 percent of the words as possible. Experiment with using fragments instead of complete sentences. Challenge yourself to create words for your characters that sound as close to a natural speaking voice as you can get.

2. Woolf advised writers to use dialogue as little as possible and only when the characters have something absolutely necessary to say. Test your own work against her advice by analyzing the dialogue of a work in progress. Ask yourself if every line is absolutely necessary. In most cases, any "hello-how-are-you, I'm-fine" dialogue can be cut—unless, of course, it happens so unusually that it reveals something important about the characters. Remind yourself that every word that comes from your character's mouth must do something: reveal character, create conflict, provide information, or move the story forward.

3. Never forget that characters in stories, like people in real life, do not always say what they mean and do not always reveal what is on their minds. Look at the last few pages of "The Window," section XIX of *To the Lighthouse* for an excellent example of dialogue that contains a terrific subtext; that is, dialogue that seems to be saying one thing on the surface but is actually communicating something quite dif-

ferent beneath. The conversation between Mr. and Mrs. Ramsay, two people who have been married for many years, seems mundane at first glance. But the subtext—the way the words actually comment on the characters' own marriage, their own love—provides the scene with a powerful undercurrent, especially when Mrs. Ramsay's final words not only heal the couple's earlier conflict but also act as an expression of her love for her husband.

4. A character's choice of words or manner of phrasing can reveal information about background, education, age, and place of birth. Create a conversation between two people who speak very differently—perhaps they are different ages or from different regions. Maintain each character's unique voice throughout the conversation.

5. Write a dialogue between two people who were in love many years ago. As they talk, let them observe to themselves the ways the other has changed or stayed the same despite the years. Let them be surprised by unexpected emotions. Let at least one of the characters resort to lies to conceal his or her real feelings.

MEMOIR

Woolf loved reading memoirs. She delighted in the quotidian details of people's lives: what they ate, how they worked, who they loved. Yet she found that many memoirs failed because they only described events and accomplishments and forgot to include "the person to whom things happened." This person to whom things happened was, of course, what interested Woolf. We go to life stories, she believed, for character, for personality. In her own memoir, "A Sketch of the Past," she does not merely describe the events of her life, but meditates on how these events shaped her character.

1. Woolf says her second memory—the sound of waves breaking on the shore—was her most important. Identify what you would consider your most important memory and write a short autobiographical sketch about it. Remember to reveal yourself by meditating on this early memory. What did this event mean to you then? How has it shaped who you are now?

2. As a way to give her readers a stronger impression of

her character in "A Sketch of the Past," Woolf entwines her memories of the past with descriptions of her present activities. For instance, she tells us she is just stepping out into the garden as she recalls her childhood visits to St. Ives. When she wonders what led her to become a writer, she also asks the question of Dickens, whose novel she is currently reading. Write a short memoir about an important event or phase in your life, but always keep your story tied to the present. See "A Sketch of the Past" for a compelling example.

3. In another autobiographical piece, "Reminiscences," Woolf blends biography and memoir. Addressed to her nephew, it is ostensibly a biography of his mother and Woolf's sister: Vanessa Bell. Woolf chronicles her childhood memories of Vanessa and details their childhood together. Write your own biographical memoir addressed to a niece or nephew describing your memory of his or her parent in childhood.

4. We all have had great seasons—that is, periods of time when we were especially passionate about some pursuit: beekeeping, horse jumping, stamp collecting. In "Hours in a Library," Woolf remembers her own "great season" of reading when she devoured classics by the shelf full. Write a memoir about your own "great season." Convey not only

your enthusiasm for the activity, but how that passion shaped your life. Consider describing both how your great season began and how it ended.

5. Woolf admired the British writer Thomas de Quincey *(Confessions of an Opium Eater)* because he felt "no obligation to recite the 'old hackneyed roll-call, chronologically arranged, of inevitable facts in a man's life.'" Write an autobiographical essay in which you avoid the "inevitable facts" of your life and convey instead a series of small, poignant recollections. Try for an effect that is fluid and dreamlike, but vivid in detail.

6. In a memoir, Woolf says of her mother, "she was one of the invisible presences who after all play so important a part in every life." Who is your invisible presence, the person behind the scenes who influences your daily life? Write a short memoir remembering that person. Explore how—for better or worse—he or she shapes who you are and how you behave. Be sure to bring this person to life for the reader: show us a living, breathing person.

7. Reviewing *The Life and Last Words of Wilfrid Ewart,* Woolf describes the book as "mainly a record of experiments in the art of growing up." Reexamine your own childhood in terms of your experiments in the art of growing up. Thinking of yourself as the artist of your childhood, write an essay that

convinces your reader that growing up is not a series of accidents, but rather is a work of art.

BIOGRAPHY

Biography was part of the air Woolf breathed. Not only had her father been the editor of the expansive *Dictionary of National Biography*, but her close friend Lytton Strachey had redefined the genre with his irreverent *Eminent Victorians*. Woolf even tried her own hand at it with a book on the life of another friend, art critic Roger Fry, as well as with her two fictional biographies, *Flush* and *Orlando*.

Yet she was never quite satisfied with the genre. It seemed, she felt, too easy to make one's subject too good, to focus too much on accomplishments and give no sense of an interior life, to offer a husk of a person and not the whole. And of course, no matter how many words a biographer might compose, the chance of capturing the complexity and fluidity of character was probably impossible—or better done with the liberties of fiction. Still, she loved to read biography and often tried to imagine innovative ways to write one.

I. Woolf says that the biographers of her age believed that "the man himself, the pith and essence of his character, shows itself to the observant eye in the tone of a voice, the turn of a head, some little phrase or anecdote picked up in passing." Write a series of very short biographical sketches—no more than a paragraph or two each—in which you try to capture your subject by identifying characteristic gestures. Use body language, gestures, tone of voice, and distinctive expressions to create a snapshot of your subject.

2. Woolf was fascinated by what she called the lives of the obscure: the life stories of people who were not famous and who did not accomplish great things. For instance, in "Life Itself," she creates a biographical account of a parson named James Woodforde who, by her own account, "was nothing in particular." In a few short pages, she reveals his character through small details of ordinary life: his view of daily events, a domestic quarrel with his niece, a passing romance, a friendship with another bachelor, and the like. Write a minibiography of someone you know; an older family member (aunt, uncle, or grandparent) works well for this exercise. The person should not be famous and should be, at least on the surface, as ordinary as possible. Select several small but significant events in the person's life that reveal his or her character as you see it. The goal is not to celebrate accomplishments, but to use the events of an ordinary life to reveal character.

3. Read the published letters of someone you admire in order to prepare to write a biographical sketch.

As you read, reflect on the material keeping alert to key events and passages that you feel reveal your subject's character. Then write a biographical sketch that captures his or her personality as you see it. Remember, you can't include everything. Analyze the material you've researched and determine how best to shape it. The difficult trick is figuring out what to bring to the foreground, what to leave in the background, and what to omit entirely without distorting the truth.

4. Write a biographical sketch of a person you think has been wrongly maligned. Do your research and create a portrait that reveals the complexity of your subject and the difficulty of his or her situation. Look at Woolf's "Eliza and Sterne" for a witty example.

5. Write a fictional biography as Woolf did in *Orlando*. Select a person you know and invent a life for him or her. For *Orlando*, Woolf imagined her friend Vita Sackville-West as a young Elizabethan nobleman who magically changes into a woman and lives three hundred years. Let your fictional biography be as fantastical as you wish, but let the setting, time, and invented character capture the essential nature of the person you know—even if all of the external features are completely different.

ESSAY

Woolf's essays are magical. Ranging in attitude from sly and clever to searching and subtle, they may be the best place to get a full appreciation of Woolf's wit and intelligence.

Writing about the art of the essay, she distinguishes one essential quality: it must give pleasure. Of course, precision of style is essential; so, too, is clarity of idea. Although artfully composed, the writing should create the impression of effortlessness. The effect of reading should be one of life intensified. While she felt that style and subject matter could range widely, any successful essay would be, she argued, "exact, truthful, and imaginative."

She held her own writing to this high standard. It was not unusual, her husband reported, for her to revise an essay five or six times before submitting it for publication. Every cadence, every metaphor, every idea, she felt, had to be tested against ear and intellect before it was acceptable.

I. The work of the greatest essayists across the centuries, according to Woolf, had one quality in common: "a fierce attachment to an idea." Because they believed something strongly, or could see something clearly, they were able to write compellingly not just for the day, Woolf would say, but for eternity. What do you believe fiercely? Base an essay on a deeply held conviction or an idea that you feel you understand with unusual clarity. Beware, Woolf would warn, against scolding or preaching.

2. Woolf felt that Max Beerbohm's great contribution to the art of the essay was to return to it the spirit of personality. In his work, she argued, he seemed to speak directly to the reader. Never preachy nor dogmatic, she observes, "he was himself, simply and directly." See if you can infuse an essay with the spirit of your personality. In it, speak familiarly to your readers, as if you know them and they know you. Create a voice that is friendly, immediate, and personal.

3. Woolf brilliantly uses metaphor and simile to excite the reader's eye, ear, and mind. For example, writing of the tendency to overly ornament one's prose, she writes, "words coagulate together in frozen sprays which, like the grapes on a Christmas-tree, glitter for a single night, but are dusty and garish the day after." Later, she talks about the essayist whose voice "comes to us not with the natural richness of the speaking voice, but strained and thin and full of mannerisms and affectations, like the voice of a man shouting through a megaphone to a crowd on a windy day." Look through essays you've already written; develop metaphors or similes that help to capture more fully the force of your ideas.

4. When describing people in essays, it is important to create crisp, compact descriptions. For example,

in *A Room of One's Own,* Woolf compresses many evocative details about the beadle who blocks her entrance to the library into a single sentence: "There issued, like a guardian angel barring the way with a flutter of black gown instead of white wings, a deprecating, silvery, kindly gentleman, who regretted in a low voice as he waved me back that ladies are only admitted to the library if accompanied by a Fellow of the College or furnished with a letter of introduction." Try writing a character description in a single sentence. Follow Woolf's lead and use physical description, simile, gesture, and voice to capture the essence of character as compactly as possible.

5. In *Three Guineas,* her long essay about how to prevent war, Woolf describes gruesome photographs of the Spanish Civil War she received in the mail. Throughout the work, she comes back to the pictures as a kind of touchstone for her argument. Write an essay whose emotional inspiration comes from a photograph. Try returning to the photo at various places to create a grounding for your ideas.

6. In nonfiction as well as in fiction, a single line of description can create a powerful impression. For instance, in a paragraph about the new aquarium at the London Zoological Gardens Woolf writes,

"Red fish, blue fish, nightmare fish, dapper fish, fish lean as gimlets, fish round and white as soup plates, ceaselessly gyrate in oblong frames of greenish light in the hushed and darkened apartment hollowed out beneath the Mappin terraces." Write freely about a place you've visited. Include as many details as come to mind. Then, once you've written it all down, select only the essential features, and distill your description to a single sentence.

7. Writing of her first impression of the soldier-poet Rupert Brooke, Woolf says, "his feet were permanently bare; he disdained tobacco and butcher's meat; and he lived all day, and perhaps slept all night, in the open air. You might judge him extreme, and from the pinnacle of superior age assure him that the return to Nature was as sophisticated as any other pose, but you could not from the first moment of speech with him doubt that, whatever he might do, he was an originator." Explore in an essay your first impression of someone extraordinary, someone you knew from the start was destined for great things.

8. Woolf's essay "On a Faithful Friend" is essentially an obituary of a dog. Although Woolf briefly recounts the dog's trials and triumphs, she also raises more searching, philosophical questions about the way people treat their pets. Although she tells us

much about dogs, she also reveals a great deal about human beings. Use an essay about a pet to reveal something about the people who own it.

9. In the first paragraph of *A Room of One's Own,* Woolf explains that "I am going to develop in your presence as fully and freely as I can the train of thought which led me to think this." Take as your subject a topic about which you hold a strong opinion. In your essay, do as Woolf did and describe the steps in thinking that brought you to your point of view. Sharing your journey with the reader should be as important as the opinion itself.

10. Early in *A Room of One's Own,* Woolf identifies various kinds of professors at Oxbridge—from the energetic to the infirm. Write a short nonfiction piece dividing a group of people into types. You might describe various kinds of bowlers, hunters, *Star Trek* fans, shoppers, stamp collectors, protesters, and so on. Describe at least four different types, but also try to identify the common bond that makes them part of the same group.

11. If you are having difficulty creating a personal voice in your essays, you might try writing it as a letter to a friend or acquaintance. In "A Letter to a Young Poet," Woolf offers advice to young writers in the form of a playful letter to a friend who wants to be a poet. Write an essay of advice in the form of a

letter to a younger person. The essay should be playful, but the topic should be serious.

12. Through the Hogarth Press, Woolf and her husband created a variety of pamphlets on numerous topics. "The Hogarth Letters" series, for example, invited writers to make their arguments in an epistolary form—that is, in letter form. Another series called the "Day to Day Pamphlets" took on contemporary issues with the goal of challenging conventional wisdom and provoking discussion. Create your own pamphlet series. Ask the members of your writing group or people in your class to contribute.

13. To prepare to write her long antiwar essay "Three Guineas," Woolf kept a notebook full of notes, newspaper clippings, and press photos. Prepare to write your own essay on a controversial subject by keeping a notebook on the topic in which you collect information that will help you make your argument. You might collect news stories, as Woolf did, opinion pieces, images, or anything else that will help you build evidence to support your view.

14. In her famous essay about modern literature "Mr. Bennett and Mrs. Brown," Woolf illustrates a point by describing two people talking on a train. She brings the people in the scene to life not merely by describing what they look like or what they are saying, but by using dialogue to let us hear their

conversation ourselves. Write a scene for an essay in progress that uses character description and dialogue to bring the argument to life.

15. "I thought how unpleasant it is to be locked out," Woolf observes in *A Room of One's Own*, "and I thought how it is worse perhaps to be locked in." Using details from your own experience and observations, explain whether it is worse to be locked out or locked in.

16. "On or about December, 1910, human character changed," Woolf extravagantly announces in "Mr. Bennett and Mrs. Brown." She explains how one began to see this change in books and in family relations. Consider in an essay how the world has changed in your lifetime. Draw examples from your own experience as well as from books, TV, theater, or anything else you can think of. Start with a bold statement like Woolf's, if you like.

17. Woolf acknowledged that whether she was writing fiction or essays, she had to think of a scene around which to focus her work. She does this in *A Room of One's Own* by contrasting two scenes: the sumptuous dinner at the men's college compared to the meager repast at the women's. Design an essay in which you use two vividly described representative scenes to demonstrate an injustice. By the conclusion of the essay, be sure to call your readers to action to remedy the situation.

18. In "How Should One Read a Book?" Woolf encourages readers to trust their own taste in books and to resist letting someone else direct their reading. Write an essay that asks a question in the title. Then, in the body of the essay, answer the question, but only by taking your reader through some unexpected twists and turns.

19. In *Mrs. Dalloway,* Clarissa hates Doris Kilman, her daughter's tutor. Use your own experience to dig deep into the emotion of hatred. What do our hatreds tell us about ourselves? About the kind of world we live in? Try to be truthful, even if that requires you to reveal something unflattering about yourself.

Virginia Woolf was of course a novelist, not a poet, so a section focusing on poetry may seem an unlikely part of this book. Yet I've included it for two reasons. First, she wrote very lyrical, poetic prose that could, in places, be called prose poetry. In fact, the novelist E. M. Forster claimed she was a poet who wrote "something as near to a novel as possible." Woolf was obviously flattered by being called a poet, but never really went so far as to claim the title for herself. In fact, she even said in a letter to a friend that "had I been able to write poetry no doubt I should have been content to leave the other alone."

The second reason it makes sense to include poetry is because Woolf was knowledgeable about it and made thoughtful observations that could be useful to poets writing today. Although she liked to assert that she couldn't be a poet because she couldn't read meter—in a playful essay called "A Letter to a Young Poet" she claims she can't tell the difference between "an iambic and a dactyl"—she was well acquainted with contemporary poetry through works published by the Hogarth Press. T. S. Eliot was a personal friend, and she greatly admired the work of W. B. Yeats. Still she felt skeptical about much of modern poetry. She appreciated its candor, but she thought its range was too limited, its technique too intellectual. In "A Letter to a Young Poet," she frames her criticism of contemporary poetry in the shape of a chatty letter to a friend and calls for poets to reconnect to the body and to the world around them.

STARTING

1. Woolf advised her nephew that an aspiring poet "must begin by being a pettifogging character, with a note book, trying to get the colour of the sunset right." The pettifogger focuses on the small, the insignificant; he quibbles about the details. Begin with an object commonly thought beautiful—a sunset, a rose—and your notebook. Write about the beauty you see, focusing not on grand themes and strong emotions, but on the smallest of details.

2. If you feel at a loss to begin a poem, start with a random prompt. For example, open a Woolf novel to any page. Write down a phrase that tantalizes your ear and use it as the first line of your poem. The poem doesn't need to have anything to do with the book—in fact, it shouldn't. Just let the phrase serve as a starting place. Don't try to figure anything out in advance; just trust your creativity and see where it takes you.

3. Begin keeping a list of questions in your notebook. Let them range from "what happened to Fluffy's cat collar?" to "what is the nature of a divine being?" When you need a writing warm-up or when

inspiration fails you, take a question from the list and answer it in a poem. Feel free to answer the same question two, three, even four or more times, developing new answers each time. Experiment by sometimes answering the question quietly and sincerely, other times fabulously or ridiculously, still other times seriously and intellectually, or even profoundly and emotionally.

4. Begin a poem with three reasons—they may range from the practical to the poetic—explaining why someone does or does not take an action. Begin each line with "since" or "because." For example, "because it was late / because she was soaking wet / because no one would notice anyway…" Notice how the repetition creates intensity and music for your opening. Let the poem follow its own course, using further repetition as you see fit. See the opening of Woolf's short story "A Summing Up" for a prose example.

5. Finding a guiding metaphor can help energize a poem. Jot down ten possible metaphors for contemporary life (for example, life is a ten-million-piece jigsaw puzzle; life is a rickety cart jostling down an uncertain road). Read through your list and find the one that has the greatest potential, and use it to open a poem. Develop the metaphor further as you go. (What happens to all those pieces of the puzzle? Does the cart sometimes get stuck or

lose a wheel?) For a superb example in prose, look at the way Woolf compares life to being "blown through the Tube at fifty miles an hour" in "The Mark on the Wall."

6. Write about a powerful emotion from a variety of angles:

    a. Offer a personal experience.
    b. Tell what your mother thinks of it.
    c. Give a scientific explanation.
    d. Suggest how it might be set to music or expressed in film.

Create the effect cumulatively, but let each section resonate with some kind of power whether it be humor, insight, music, or imagery.

THE SENSES AND THE WORLD

Woolf felt hers was a great age for lyric poetry, but encouraged modern poets to reach further. Though the lyric poem might be emotionally powerful, she felt it focused too much on the individual, too much on the self. She challenged poets to rediscover the richness of the English language, the power of the senses, and bounty of the outside world.

I. Sometimes, Woolf lamented, modern poets were too abstract and intellectual. They wrote "as if they had neither ears nor eyes, neither soles to their feet nor palms to their hands." Practice infusing the senses into your language by writing a five-stanza poem about a place that has some significance to you—it can be a city, a town, a mountain lake, or a patch of grass in a vacant lot. In each stanza, explore the place using one sense. Stanza one might describe sight; stanza two sound; stanza three taste; stanza four touch; stanza five smell. Let each sense bring its own kind of life to your poem.

2. Poets, Woolf suggests, need to stop sitting alone in their rooms with the curtains drawn and get out into the world. Take her at her word by visiting your local discount store or chain store. Notice the width of the aisles, the array of smells, the softness or violence of the light, the shapes and names of the merchandise. When you get home, write a poem using what you've observed to capture the ambience of the place. Imagine that your poem will be the only record of its existence long after the store has disappeared.

3. Write a poem in which you make sense of the chaos or hubbub of your life. Look for, as Woolf puts it, "the relation between things that seem incompatible yet have a mysterious affinity."

4. Woolf scorned the idea that "science has made poetry impossible; there is no poetry in motor cars and wireless." Look for the poetry in science or technology by writing a celebratory poem about an-

tibiotics, X-ray machines, microscopes, space shuttles, motherboards—whatever machines or inventions you find around you that inspire you to praise modern life.

5. "There is nothing to take the place of childhood," a character thinks in Woolf's story "Mrs. Dalloway in Bond Street." "A leaf of mint brings it back: or a cup with a blue ring." In your notebook, recall objects from your childhood. Once you begin writing them down, you'll soon start remembering things you thought you'd forgotten long ago. Try to identify at least twenty items, more if possible. Write a poem or series of poems about your childhood based on the most poignant items from your list.

CHARACTERS

Woolf believed that developing and using characters in poetry was essential, not just to expand the scope of the poem, but to improve a poet's facility with language. By imagining they are someone else and speaking in someone else's voice, she says, writers learn the richness and variety of English. Writers who experiment with a wide range of characters will learn how to have the entire language at their disposal.

1. To practice developing characters in poetry, Woolf advises poets to "embark upon a long poem in

which people as unlike yourself as possible talk at the tops of their voices." To try out other people's voices in poems, begin by writing a series of dramatic monologues. A dramatic monologue is simply a poem written in the voice of an invented character. For example, you could write a monologue from the point of view of an elderly woman whose Social Security check has been stolen, or from the perspective of a boy who has just gone to school for the first time. As Woolf advises, imagine people as unlike yourself as possible for this exercise. Imagine yourself into their bodies, experiences, consciousnesses. Imagine the words, phrasing, references, and ideas your character would be likely to use. The monologue, of course, originated in theatrical monologues, so once you are finished, try reading it aloud.

2. Woolf instructs poets to create "characters not spun out at length in the novelist's way, but condensed and synthesised in the poet's way." Experiment with capturing character in a "condensed" form by writing five very short poems (no more than ten lines each) about five different people. Explore the way gesture, language, and appearance can capture the essence of character in a very short space.

3. Write a poem from the point of view of a man or woman who desires a different body. You might begin with the obvious, the middle-aged man who

wants to be young again, but also experiment with the less likely: a beautiful woman longing to be plain.

4. Using alternating points of view, write a poem in which you describe two people meeting for a blind date. You might begin with one person seeing the other sitting in the café; then shift to the person inside who is beginning to get nervous about the meeting. Throughout the poem, shift between the two perspectives.

5. To experiment with unusual perspectives in a poem, alternate the comments of a Greek chorus—that is, a group of characters who comment on the subject of the poem, but who have no direct involvement with the action—with the voice of the main speaker.

6. Spinning off from some advice Woolf gives in *A Room of One's Own*, write a poem in which a character meditates on his or her beauty or plainness. Writing a long poem—say two pages—will require that you delve deeply into the topic.

EXPERIMENTS: SATIRE, COMEDY, REVOLT, MEMORY

Woolf lamented the demise of satire and comedy in poetry; she longed for poetry that could shame readers for their transgressions or make them laugh out loud.

1. To revive satire and social critique in poetry, identify a form of hypocrisy and take a stand in a poem against it. Experiment with all kinds of ways to attack the hypocrisy: try scornful wit or exaggeration; perhaps irony or understatement; or even logical argument.

2. Experiment with hyperbole or exaggeration as a way to create a comic effect. Write a poem that exaggerates the qualities of an insignificant thing like an ant or a spitball. Be so extravagant, so over the top, that you make us laugh.

3. Write a poem in response to something that enrages you. The idea here is to experiment with the power and energy of words. Make violent accusations, speak truth to power. Don't constrain yourself; be unreasonable, unfair, and childish, but above all, unleash intensity.

4. Another way to bring comedy to poetry is to approach the revered irreverently. For example, in her novel *Flush*, Woolf retells the story of the famous love affair between the poets Robert Browning and Elizabeth Barrett Browning from the point of view of their spaniel. Write a poem in which you retell a famous story from the point of view of an animal. It can be an animal that actually lived (like Lewis and Clark's Newfoundland, Seaman) or simply an imagined animal (a flea aboard the space shuttle). Let your imagination soar.

5. Woolf famously wrote in *A Room of One's Own* that we "think back through our mothers if we are women." If you are a woman, write a poem about your "mothers"; that is, the women—related to you or not—who have helped to create the person you are today. If you are a man, write a poem in the same vein about your "fathers."

BIBLIOGRAPHY

Gordon, Lyndall. *Virginia Woolf: A Writer's Life.* Oxford: Oxford University Press, 1984.

Lee, Hermione. *Virginia Woolf.* London: Chatto & Windus, 1996.

Noble, Joan Russell, ed. *Recollections of Virginia Woolf.* London: Peter Owen, 1972.

Stape, J. H., ed. *Virginia Woolf: Interviews and Recollections.* Iowa City: University of Iowa Press, 1995.

Woolf, Virginia. *A Room of One's Own.* San Diego: Harcourt Brace & Company, 1929. Reprinted with foreword by Mary Gordon. San Diego: Harvest, 1989. (Page references are to the 1989 edition.)

————. *A Writer's Diary: Being Extracts from The Diary of Virginia Woolf.* Ed. Leonard Woolf. New York: Harvest/Harcourt Brace Jovanovich, 1954.

————. *Books and Portraits: Some Further Selections from the Literary and Biographical Writings of Virginia Woolf.* Ed. Mary Lyon. New York: Harvest/Harcourt Brace Jovanovich, 1977.

————. *The Captain's Death Bed and Other Essays.* New York: Harvest/Harcourt Brace Jovanovich, 1950.

————. *The Common Reader: First Series.* New York: Harvest/Harcourt Brace Jovanovich, 1925.

————. *The Complete Shorter Fiction.* Ed. Susan Dick. London: Triad Grafton Books, 1987.

————. *The Death of the Moth and Other Essays.* San Diego: Harvest/Harcourt Brace & Company, 1942.

————. *The Diary of Virginia Woolf.* Ed. Anne Olivier Bell. Vol. II (1920–1924). San Diego: Harcourt Brace Jovanovich, Inc., 1978.

————. *The Diary of Virginia Woolf.* Ed. Anne Olivier Bell. Vol. III (1925–1930). San Diego: Harcourt Brace Jovanovich, Inc., 1980.

————. *The Diary of Virginia Woolf.* Ed. Anne Olivier Bell. Vol. IV (1931–1935). San Diego: Harcourt Brace & Company, 1982.

————. *The Essays of Virginia Woolf.* Ed. Andrew McNeillie. Vol. III (1919–1924). San Diego: Harcourt Brace Jovanovich, 1988.

————. *Granite and Rainbow.* San Diego: Harvest/Harcourt Brace Jovanovich, 1958.

————. *The Letters of Virginia Woolf.* Eds. Nigel Nicolson and Joanne Trautmann. Vol. III: 1923–1928. New York: Harcourt Brace Jovanovich, 1977.

————. *The Letters of Virginia Woolf.* Eds. Nigel Nicolson and Joanne Trautmann. Vol. V: 1932–1935. New York: Harcourt Brace Jovanovich, Inc., 1979.

———. *The London Scene: Five Essays by Virginia Woolf.* New York: Random House, 1975.

———. *The Moment and Other Essays.* New York: Harvest/Harcourt Brace Jovanovich, 1948.

———. *Moments of Being.* Ed. Jeanne Schulkind. 2nd ed. San Diego: Harvest/Harcourt Brace Jovanovich, 1985.

———. *Mrs. Dalloway's Party: A Short Story Sequence.* Ed. Stella McNichol. New York: Harvest/Harcourt Brace Jovanovich, 1973.

———. *The Pargiters. The Novel-Essay Portion of* The Years. Ed. Mitchell A. Leaska. London: The Hogarth Press, 1978.

———. *The Second Common Reader.* San Diego: Harcourt Brace Jovanovich, 1932. Reprint. Ed. Andrew McNeillie. San Diego: Harcourt Brace Jovanovich, 1986. (Page references are to the 1986 edition.)

———. *To the Lighthouse.* San Diego: Harcourt Brace Jovanovich, 1927. Reprinted with a foreword by Eudora Welty. Harvest/Harcourt Brace Jovanovich, 1981. (Page references are to the 1981 edition.)

———. *To the Lighthouse.* San Diego: Harcourt Brace Jovanovich, 1927. Reprinted with annotations and introduction by Mark Hussey. Orlando: Harvest/Harcourt, 2005.

NOTES

If not otherwise indicated, citations are from Virginia Woolf.

PREFACE

5 "The light of the English language a little further against
darkness": E. M. Forster quoted in *Recollections of Virginia Woolf,*
Joan Russell Noble, 198.
6 "To sacrifice a hair of the head of your vision, a shade of its
colour, in deference to some Headmaster with a silver pot in
his hand or to some professor with a measuring-rod up his
sleeve, is the most abject treachery": *A Room of One's Own,* 106.

PRACTICING

9 "A room of her own and five hundred a year": *A Room of One's
Own,* 94.

9   "Wants life to proceed with the utmost quiet and regularity. He wants to see the same faces, to read the same books, to do the same things day after day, month after month . . . so that nothing may disturb or disquiet the mysterious nosings about, feelings round, darts, dashes and sudden discoveries of that very shy and illusive spirit, the imagination": "Professions for Women," *The Death of the Moth and Other Essays,* 239.

10 "I hope I am not giving away professional secrets if I say that a novelist's chief desire is to be as unconscious as possible": Ibid.

10 "Imagine me writing a novel in a state of trance": Ibid., 240.

10 "Fisherman lying sunk in dreams on the verge of a deep lake with a rod held out over the water . . . imagination sweep unchecked round every rock and cranny of the world that lies submerged in the depths of our unconscious being": Ibid.

12 "Had I not killed her she would have killed me. She would have plucked the heart out of my writing.": Ibid., 238.

12 "She died hard. . . . She was always creeping back when I thought I had despatched her.": Ibid.

12 "Her fictitious nature was of great assistance to her.": Ibid.

12 "Such a good morning's writing I'd planned . . . wasted the cream of my brain on the telephone": *The Diary of Virginia Woolf,* Vol. II, 32.

13 "Nonsense by the ream. Be silly, be sentimental, imitate Shelley . . . give the rein to every impulse; commit every fault of style, grammar, taste, and syntax; pour out; tumble over; loose anger, love, satire, in whatever words you can catch, coerce or create, in whatever metre, prose, poetry, or gibberish that

comes to hand. Thus you will learn to write": "A Letter to a Young Poet," *The Death of the Moth and Other Essays*, 224.

13 "The habit of writing thus for my own eye only is good practice.": *A Writer's Diary*, 13.

15 "It is a disgrace that I write nothing, or if I write, write sloppily": Ibid., 65.

15 "I must learn to write more succinctly.... I am horrified by my own looseness": Ibid., 140.

15 "I am now writing as fast and freely as I have written the whole of my life; more so—20 times more so—than any novel yet": Ibid., 84.

16 "I do feel fairly sure that I am grazing as near as I can to my own ideas, and getting a tolerable shape for them...But I have my ups and downs": Ibid., 69.

WORKING

19 For information about how much five hundred pounds might be today, see Hermione Lee, *Virginia Woolf*, 557.

20 "I prefer, where truth is important, to write fiction": *The Partigers*, 9.

20 "Mrs. Behn was a middle-class woman...forced by the death of her husband and some unfortunate adventures of her own to make her living by her wits": *A Room of One's Own*, 63.

21 "A very glorious day it was for me": "Professions for Women," *The Death of the Moth and Other Essays*, 236.

22 "I have to admit that instead of spending that sum upon

bread and butter, rent, shoes and stockings, or butcher's bills, I went out and bought a cat—a beautiful cat, a Persian cat, which very soon involved me in bitter disputes with my neighbours": Ibid.

22 "What could be easier than to write articles and to buy Persian cats with the profits?": Ibid.

23 "The habit of freedom and the courage to write exactly what we think": *A Room of One's Own*, 113.

23 "Even allowing a generous margin for symbolism, that five hundred a year stands for the power to contemplate, that a lock on the door means the power to think for oneself": Ibid., 106.

26 "A faculty for housing themselves appropriately, for making the table, the chair, the curtain, the carpet into their own image": *The London Scene*, 23.

CREATING

29 "So long as you write what you wish to write, that is all that matters": *A Room of One's Own*, 106.

29 "Write exactly as you think—that is the only way": *Letters of Virginia Woolf*, Vol. VI, 259.

29 "Examine for a moment an ordinary mind on an ordinary day. The mind receives a myriad impressions—trivial, fantastic, evanescent, or engraved with the sharpness of steel": "Modern Fiction," *The Common Reader: First Series*, 154.

29 "Let us record the atoms as they fall upon the mind in the order in which they fall, let us trace the pattern": Ibid., 155.

30 "Writers are infinitely sensitive; each writer has a different sensibility": "The Leaning Tower," *The Moment and Other Essays*, 130.

30 "Sometimes at country fairs you may have seen a professor on a platform exhorting the peasants to come up and buy his wonder-working pills. Whatever their disease, whether of body or mind, he has a name for it and a cure; and if they hang back in doubt he whips out a diagram and points with a stick at different parts of the human anatomy, and gabbles so quickly such long Latin words that first one shyly stumbles forward and then another, and takes his bolus and carries it away and unwraps it secretly and swallows it in hope": "The Anatomy of Fiction," *Granite and Rainbow*, 53.

31 "And receive ... five pills together with nine suggestions for home treatment. In other words they are given five 'review questions' to answer, and are advised to read nine books or parts of books": Ibid.

31 "The realistic method": Ibid.

31 "A bundle of testimonials to the miraculous nature of his cures. But let us consider ... we are not credulous ploughboys; and fiction is not a disease": Ibid.

32 "In England we have been in the habit of saying that fiction is an art": Ibid.

32 "Every work of art can be taken to pieces, and those pieces can be named and numbered, divided and subdivided, and

given their order of precedence, like the internal organs of a frog": Ibid., 54.

32 "The complication, the major knot, and the explication": Ibid.

32 "Emphasis by terminal position, by initial position, by pause, by direct proportion": Ibid., 55.

32 "You may dissect your frog, but you cannot make it hop": Ibid.

32 "Nobody knows anything about the laws of fiction...We can only trust our instincts": "The Art of Fiction," *The Moment and Other Essays,* 110.

32 "Any method is right, every method is right, that expresses what we wish to express, if we are writers": "Modern Fiction," 156.

32 "No 'method,' no experiment, even of the wildest—is forbidden": Ibid., 158.

33 "Be truthful...and the result is bound to be amazingly interesting": *A Room of One's Own,* 91.

33 "Whether it matters for ages or only for hours": Ibid., 106.

33 "It is much more important to be oneself than anything else": Ibid., 111.

33 "Write daily; write freely; but let us always compare what we have written with what the great writers have written. It is humiliating, but it is essential": "The Leaning Tower," 153.

34 "The writer then would submit his work to the judge of his choice; an appointment would be made; an interview arranged. In strict privacy, and with some formality—the fee, however, would be enough to ensure that the interview did not

degenerate into tea-table gossip—doctor and writer would meet; and for an hour they would consult upon the book in question. They would talk, seriously and privately": "Reviewing," *The Captain's Death Bed and Other Essays*, 138.

35 "A well-stored mind, housing other books and even other literatures": Ibid., 139.

35 "The art of writing is difficult; at every stage the opinion of an impersonal and disinterested critic would be of the highest value": Ibid., 139.

35 "Who would not spout the family teapot in order to talk with Keats for an hour about poetry, or with Jane Austen about the art of fiction?": Ibid., 140.

WALKING

39 "Passionately towards a lead pencil": "Street Haunting," *The Death of the Moth and Other Essays*, 20.

39 "Under cover of this excuse, we could indulge safely in the greatest pleasure of town life in winter—rambling the streets of London": Ibid.

39 "Part of that vast republican army of anonymous trampers": Ibid.

40 "Walking through the long grass in the meadows": *The Diary of Virginia Woolf*, Vol. II, 176.

40 "The silver sheep clustering; & the downs soaring. It feeds me, rests me, satisfies me, as nothing else does... This has a holiness": *The Diary of Virginia Woolf*, vol. 4, 124.

40 "I have been in such a haze and dream and intoxication, declaiming phrases, seeing scenes, as I walk": *A Writer's Diary*, 183.

40 "In fine writing trim": Ibid., 29.

41 "Nosing along, making up phrases": *The Letters of Virginia Woolf*, Vol. III, 241.

41 "Space to spread my mind out": *The Diary of Virginia Woolf*, Vol. III, 107.

41 "The loveliest country in the world, with the corn ripening, and yellow butterflies": *The Letters of Virginia Woolf*, Vol. V, 88.

READING

45 "The only advice…that one person can give another about reading is to take no advice…to follow your own instincts, to use your own reason, to come to your own conclusions": "How Should One Read a Book?" *The Second Common Reader*, 258.

45 "Independence which is the most important quality a reader can possess": Ibid.

45 "Each of us has an appetite that must find for itself the food that nourishes it": "The Leaning Tower," *The Moment and Other Essays*, 154.

46 "Reading omnivorously, simultaneously, poems, plays, novels, histories, biographies, the old and the new": Ibid.

46 "Devouring books, almost faster than I like": Leslie Stephen quoted in Lyndall Gordon, *Virginia Woolf: A Writer's Life*, 74.

46 "She takes in a great deal & will really be an author in time": Ibid., 15.

46 "Let us bear in mind a piece of advice that an eminent Victorian who was also an eminent pedestrian once gave to walkers: 'Whenever you see a board up with "Trespassers will be prosecuted," trespass at once'.... Literature is no one's private ground; literature is common ground": "The Leaning Tower," 154.

47 "Nor let us shy away from the kings because we are commoners...Read me, read me for yourselves": Ibid.

47 "A love of literature is often roused and...nourished not by the good books, but by the bad": "Gothic Romance," *Granite and Rainbow*, 58.

47 "Reached the age of thirty without writing his autobiography": "The Leaning Tower," 148.

48 "Consider how difficult it is to tell the truth about one-self...to admit that one is petty, vain, mean, frustrated, tortured, unfaithful, and unsuccessful": Ibid.

48 "You must illumine your own soul with its profundities and its shallows, and its vanities and its generosities, and say what your beauty means to you or your plainness": *A Room of One's Own*, 90.

49 "Some fierce attachment to an idea. It is on the back of an idea, something believed in with conviction or seen with precision": "The Modern Essay," *The Common Reader: First Series*, 227.

49 "The essay must be pure—pure like water or pure like wine, but pure from dullness, deadness, and deposits of extraneous matter": Ibid., 218.

49 "To sting us wide awake and fix us in a trance which is not sleep but rather an intensification of life": Ibid., 217.

49 "The principle which controls it...that it should give pleasure. It should lay us under a spell with its first word, and we should only wake, refreshed, with its last": Ibid., 216.

49 "Least calls for the use of long words": Ibid.

49 "Admits more properly than biography or fiction of sudden boldness and metaphor": Ibid., 219.

49 "Can be polished till every atom of its surface shines...like the grapes on a Christmas-tree, glitter for a single night, but are dusty and garish the day after": Ibid.

50 "Wild flash of imagination, that lightning crack of genius in the middle...which leaves them flawed and imperfect, but starred with poetry": *A Room of One's Own,* 7.

50 "The spirit of personality permeates every word...is the triumph of style": "The Modern Essay," 222.

50 "The weighing of cadences, the consideration of pauses; the effect of repetitions and consonances and assonances—all this was...the duty of a writer who wishes to put a complex meaning fully and completely before his reader": "DeQuincey's Autobiography," *The Second Common Reader,* 134.

51 " 'Read a little Shakespeare'...'to loosen my muscles' ": *A Writer's Diary,* 243.

51 "I have sometimes dreamt...that when the Day of Judgment dawns and the great conquerors and lawyers and statesmen come to receive their rewards—their crowns, their laurels, their names carved indelibly upon imperishable

marble—the Almighty will turn to Peter and will say, not without a certain envy when He sees us coming with our books under our arms, 'Look, these need no reward. We have nothing to give them here. They have loved reading' ": "How Should One Read a Book?" *The Second Common Reader*, 270.

PUBLISHING

55 "Publish nothing before you are thirty": "A Letter to a Young Poet," *The Death of the Moth and Other Essays*, 224.

55 "If you publish your freedom will be checked; you will be thinking what people will say; you will write for others when you ought only to be writing for yourself": Ibid., 225.

56 "Found out how to begin...to say something in my own voice": *A Writer's Diary*, 46.

57 "I could go on writing like that—the tug and suck are at me to do it": Ibid., 36.

58 "The only woman in England free to write what I like": Ibid., 81.

59 "It must be like taking the veil and entering a religious order—observing the rites and rigours of metre": "A Letter to a Young Poet," 210.

59 "Could one say what one meant and observe the rules of poetry?": Ibid., 210.

60 "A poet's prose": Rose Macaulay quoted in J. H. Stape, ed., *Virginia Woolf*, 181.

60 "Gives expression to sensation more vigorously, more

exactly than we can manage for ourselves in the flesh. It is a world of astonishing physical brilliance and intensity; sharpened, intensified as objects are in a clearer air; such as we see them, not in dreams, but when all the faculties are alert and vigorous": "The Faery Queen," *The Moment and Other Essays*, 30.

60 "Under the more intense ray of poetry; under its sharper, its lovelier light": Ibid.

60 "Modern poets... have all the virtues, and none of the gifts": *The Letters of Virginia Woolf*, Vol. V, 22.

60 "The lyric cry of ecstasy or despair, which is so intense, so personal, and so limited, is not enough": "Narrow Bridge of Art," *Granite and Rainbow*, 12.

61 "In poetry you get greater intensity than in prose, and have the right to be more jerky and disconnected. But I think you carry this right a little far. These are the chief criticisms I have to make; too much detail; too jerky; not sufficiently seen as a whole. On the other side; vividness; truthfulness, and often some striking observation": *The Letters of Virginia Woolf*, Vol. III, 432.

61 "Incredible though this now seems... you made us roar with laughter... later, you were lashing our follies, trouncing our hypocrisies, and dashing off the most brilliant of satires": "A Letter to a Young Poet," 220.

61 "It is apparently easier to write a poem about oneself than about any other subject": Ibid., 217.

62 "Let your rhythmical sense wind itself in and out among men and women, omnibuses, sparrows—whatever comes [*sic*]

along the street—until it has strung them together in one harmonious whole": Ibid., 221.

62 "Re-think human life into poetry and so give us tragedy again and comedy by means of characters, not spun out at length in the novelist's way, but condensed and synthesised in the poet's way": Ibid.

62 "The art of having at one's beck and call every word in the language, of knowing their weights, colours, sounds, associations, and thus making them . . . suggest more than they can state . . . effectively by imagining that one is not oneself but somebody different": Ibid., 223.

62 "You will do well to embark upon a long poem in which people as unlike yourself as possible talk at the tops of their voices": Ibid., 224.

63 "Publish nothing before you are thirty": Ibid.

63 "They wont [sic] spoil with keeping": *The Letters of Virginia Woolf*, Vol. V, 83.

65 "Succeed . . . by simplifying: practically everything is left out": *A Writer's Diary*, 136.

DOUBTING

67 "The novelist . . . is terribly exposed to life. . . . Taste, sound, movement, a few words here, a gesture there, a man coming in, a woman going out, even the motor that passes in the street or the beggar who shuffles along the pavement, and all the reds

and blues and lights and shades of the scene claim his attention.... can no more cease to receive impressions than a fish in mid-ocean can cease to let the water rush through his gills": "Life and the Novelist," *Granite and Rainbow*, 41.

68   "Life is forever pleading that she is the proper end of fiction...the more he sees of her and catches of her the better his book will be. She does not add...that the side she flaunts uppermost is often, for the novelist, of no value whatever": Ibid., 46.

68   "The writer's task is to take one thing and let it stand for twenty": Ibid., 45.

68   "Each sentence must have, at its heart, a little spark of fire, and this, whatever the risk, the novelist must pluck with his own hands from the blaze": Ibid., 47.

69   "The main thing in beginning a novel is to feel, not that you can write it, but that it exists on the far side of a gulf, which words can't cross: that its [*sic*] to be pulled through only in a breathless anguish...A novel, to be good, should seem, before one writes it, something unwriteable": *The Letters of Virginia Woolf*, Vol. III, 529.

70   "One element remains constant in all novels, and that is the human element...they excite in us the feelings that people excite in us in real life": "Phases of Fiction," *Granite and Rainbow*, 141.

70   "The English writer would...bring out her oddities and mannerisms; her buttons and wrinkles; her ribbons and warts. Her personality would dominate the book. A French writer

would rub out all that; he would sacrifice the individual Mrs. Brown to give a more general view of human nature; to make a more abstract, proportioned, and harmonious whole. The Russian would pierce through the flesh; would reveal the soul—the soul alone, wandering out into the Waterloo Road, asking of life some tremendous question which would sound on and on in our ears after the book was finished": "Mr. Bennett and Mrs. Brown," *The Captain's Death Bed and Other Essays,* 102.

71 "Be chary of dialogue because dialogue puts the most violent pressure upon the reader's attention": "An Essay in Criticism," *Granite and Rainbow,* 91.

71 "To preserve more sincerely and exactly what interests and moves them, even if to do so they must discard most of the conventions which are commonly observed by the novelist": "Modern Fiction," *The Common Reader: First Series,* 150.

72 "We are aware of relations and subtleties which have not yet been explored": "Phases of Fiction," *Granite and Rainbow,* 145.

72 "We scarcely know what powers it may not hold concealed within it": Ibid.

72 "I am by no means confining you to fiction . . . write books of travel and adventure, and research and scholarship, and history and biography, and criticism and philosophy and science. Write all kinds of books, hesitating at no subject however trivial or however vast": *A Room of One's Own,* 109.

72 "Is it nonsense, is it brilliance?": *A Writer's Diary,* 87.

72 "Is the greatest rapture known to me": Ibid., 115.

73 "I prefer, where truth is important, to write fiction": *The Pargiters*, 9.

73 "There it was—her picture. Yes, with all its greens and blues, its lines running up and across, its attempt at something. It would be hung in the attics, she thought; it would be destroyed. But what did that matter? she asked herself, taking up her brush again. She looked at the steps; they were empty; she looked at her canvas; it was blurred. With a sudden intensity, as if she saw it clear for a second, she drew a line there, in the centre. It was done; it was finished. Yes, she thought, laying down her brush in extreme fatigue, I have had my vision": *To the Lighthouse*, 208.

SPARKS

81 "Commoners and outsiders": "The Leaning Tower," *The Moment and Other Essays*, 154.

81 "We teach ourselves how to read and to write, how to preserve, and how to create": Ibid.

FICTION SPARKS

85 "To begin reading with a pen in my hand, discovering, pouncing, thinking of phrases, when the ground is new, remains one of my great excitements": *A Writer's Diary*, 147.

85 "One must begin by being chaotic": Ibid., 68.

87 "I can make up situations, but I cannot make up plots":
Ibid., 114.

87 "Two blocks joined by a corridor": quoted in the
introduction by Mark Hussey, *To the Lighthouse*, xxxix.

88 "Without knowing I do it, instantly make up a scene": *A
Writer's Diary*, 114.

89 "States the essential and lets the reader do the rest...reader
with every possible help and suggestion": Ibid., 203.

93 "How I dig out beautiful caves behind my characters: I
think that gives exactly what I want; humanity, humour,
depth": Ibid., 59.

94 "Very clearly Greek, straight, blue-eyed": *To the Lighthouse*, 29.

94 "Chinese eyes": Ibid., 17.

95 "Sympathy with humble things": Ibid., 21.

96 "Tinselly": *A Writer's Diary*, 77.

98 "Made to feel violently two opposite things at the same
time": *To the Lighthouse*, 102.

100 " 'Yes, of course, if it's fine tomorrow,' said Mrs. Ramsay.
'But you'll have to be up with the lark,' she added....
" 'But,' said his father...'it won't be fine.'...
" 'But it may be fine—I expect it will be fine,' said Mrs.
Ramsay, making some little twist of the reddish-brown
stocking she was knitting, impatiently....
" 'It's due west,' said...Tansley, holding his bony fingers spread
so that the wind blew through them ...
" 'Nonsense,' said Mrs. Ramsay....

" 'There'll be no landing at the Lighthouse tomorrow,' said Charles Tansley, clapping his hands together.…

" 'No going to the Lighthouse, James.' …

" 'Perhaps you will wake up and find the sun shining and the birds singing,' she said compassionately, smoothing the little boy's hair.… 'Perhaps it will be fine tomorrow.' " : Ibid., 3–15.

103   "We perish, each alone": Ibid., 169.

NONFICTION SPARKS

106   "The person to whom things happened": *Moments of Being*, 65.

108   "No obligation to recite 'the old hackneyed roll-call, chronologically arranged, of inevitable facts in a man's life' ": "Impassioned Prose," *Granite and Rainbow*, 37.

108   "She was one of the invisible presences who after all play so important a part in every life": *Moments of Being*, 80.

108   "Mainly a record of experiments in the art of growing up": *The Essays of Virginia Woolf,* Vol. III, 409.

109   "The man himself, the pith and essence of his character, shows itself to the observant eye in the tone of a voice, the turn of a head, some little phrase or anecdote picked up in passing": "The New Biography," *Granite and Rainbow*, 153.

110   "Was nothing in particular": "Two Parsons," *The Second Common Reader,* 95.

111   "Eliza and Sterne": *Granite and Rainbow,* 176.

112   "Exact, truthful, and imaginative": "The Modern Essay," *The Common Reader: First Series,* 226.

112 "A fierce attachment to an idea": Ibid., 227.

113 "He was himself, simply and directly": Ibid., 222.

113 "Words coagulate together in frozen sprays which, like the grapes on a Christmas-tree, glitter for a single night, but are dusty and garish the day after": Ibid., 219.

113 "Not with the natural richness of the speaking voice, but strained and thin and full of mannerisms and affectations, like the voice of a man shouting through a megaphone to a crowd on a windy day": Ibid., 224.

114 "There issued, like a guardian angel barring the way with a flutter of black gown instead of white wings, a deprecating, silvery, kindly gentleman, who regretted in a low voice as he waved me back that ladies are only admitted to the library if accompanied by a Fellow of the College or furnished with a letter of introduction": *A Room of One's One*, 7.

115 "Red fish, blue fish, nightmare fish, dapper fish, fish lean as gimlets, fish round and white as soup plates, ceaselessly gyrate in oblong frames of greenish light in the hushed and darkened apartment hollowed out beneath the Mappin terraces": *The Essays of Virginia Woolf*, Vol. III, 404.

115 "His feet were permanently bare; he disdained tobacco and butcher's meat; and he lived all day, and perhaps slept all night, in the open air. You might judge him extreme, and from the pinnacle of superior age assure him that the return to Nature was as sophisticated as any other pose, but you could not from the first moment of speech with him doubt that, whatever he might do, he was an originator": *Books and Portraits*, 86.

115 "On a Faithful Friend," Ibid., 10.

116 "I am going to develop in your presence as fully and freely
as I can the train of thought which led me to think this": *A
Room of One's Own*, 4.

118 "I thought how unpleasant it is to be locked out; and
I thought how it is worse perhaps to be locked in": Ibid.,
24.

118 "On or about December, 1910, human character
changed": "Mr. Bennett and Mrs. Brown," *The Captain's Death
Bed and Other Essays*, 96.

120 "Something as near to a novel as possible": E. M. Forster,
quoted in *Recollections of Virginia Woolf*, Joan Russell Noble, ed., 193.

POETRY SPARKS

120 "Had I been able to write poetry no doubt I should have
been content to leave the other alone": *The Letters of Virginia Woolf*,
Vol. V, 317.

120 "An iambic and a dactyl": "A Letter to a Young Poet," *The
Death of a Moth and Other Essays*, 210.

121 "One must begin by being a pettifogging character, with a
note book, trying to get the colour of the sunset right": *The
Letters of Virginia Woolf*, Vol. III, 491.

123 "Blown through the Tube at fifty miles an hour": "The
Mark on the Wall," *Virginia Woolf: The Complete Shorter Fiction*, 110.

123 "As if they had neither ears nor eyes, neither soles to their
feet nor palms to their hands": "A Letter to a Young Poet,"
222.

124 "The relation between things that seem incompatible yet have a mysterious affinity": Ibid., 221.

124 "Science . . . has made poetry impossible; there is no poetry in motor cars and wireless": Ibid., 220.

125 "There is nothing to take the place of childhood. A leaf of mint brings it back: or a cup with a blue ring": "Mrs. Dalloway in Bond St.," *Mrs. Dalloway's Party: A Short Story Sequence,* 19.

125 "Embark upon a long poem in which people as unlike yourself as possible talk at the tops of their voices": "A Letter to a Young Poet," 224.

126 "Characters not spun out at length in the novelist's way, but condensed and synthesised in the poet's way": Ibid., 221.

129 "For we think back through our mothers if we are women": *A Room of One's Own,* 76.

INDEX

Afterwords: Letters on the Death of Virginia Woolf (Oldfield), 78–79

Angel in the House, 12, 16–17

Auden, W. H., 59

Austen, Jane, 33, 35

Banks, Joan Trautmann, 78

Beerbohm, Max, 113

Behn, Aphra, 20–21

Bell, Quentin, 79

Bell, Vanessa, 24, 107

biography, 109–12

Bloomsbury group, 5, 24, 78, 84–85

Books and Portraits (Woolf), 115; "On a Faithful Friend," 115

Brontë, Charlotte, 34

Brontë parsonage, 24

Brooke, Rupert, 26, 115

Browning, Elizabeth Barrett, 77, 128

Browning, Robert, 128

Byron, George Gordon, Lord, 41

Captain's Death Bed and Other Essays, The (Woolf): "Mr. Bennett and Mrs. Brown," 70, 117, 118; "Reviewing," 34–35

character, 62, 70–71, 74–76, 85, 93–98; actions, 94; in essays, 117–18; interior thoughts, 93–94; living spaces, 94; minor, 98; others' descriptions, 94; others' thoughts, 95; in poetry, 125–27. *See also* nonfiction sparks: memoir

Common Reader, The: First Series (Woolf): "The Modern Essay," 49, 50, 111, 112, 113; "Modern Fiction," 29, 32, 71

Confessions of an Opium Eater (de Quincey), 108

conflict, 89–90

Congenial Spirits: The Selected Letters of Virginia Woolf (Banks, ed.), 78

Death of the Moth and Other Essays, The (Woolf): "A Letter to a Young Poet," 13, 56, 59, 61–63, 116, 120, 123, 124, 125, 126; "Professions for Women," 4, 9, 10, 12, 21–22, 78; "Street Haunting," 27, 37, 43

de Quincey, Thomas, 108

dialogue, 71, 74, 103–5, 117–18

Diary of Virginia Woolf, The: Vol. II, 12, 40; Vol. III and IV, 40

diary or journal keeping, 13–16, 17–18, 51, 85

Dick, Susan, 123

Dickens, Charles, 107

Dictionary of National Biography (Stephen, ed.), 109

Donne, John, 33

Dostoyevsky, Fyodor, 58, 89

doubting oneself, 72–73

Eliot, T. S., 58–59, 78, 120

Eminent Victorians (Strachey), 109

Empson, William, 59

essay, 48–51, 112–19

Essays of Virginia Woolf, The, Vol. III, 108, 115

fiction sparks: beginnings, 84–87; character, 93–98; conflict, 90–93; dialogue, 103–5; point of view and narration, 99–102; scene, 88–90; setting, 102–3; structure, 87–88

Flush (Woolf), 33, 77, 109, 128

Forster, E. M., 5, 58, 78, 120

Freud, Sigmund, 58

Fry, Roger, 109

Gordon, Lyndall, 46, 79

Gorky, Maxim, 58

Granite and Rainbow (Woolf): "The Anatomy of Fiction," 30–32; "Eliza and Sterne," 111; "An Essay in Criticism," 71; "Gothic Romance," 47; "Impassioned Prose," 108; "Life and the Novelist," 67, 68; "Narrow Bridge of Art," 60; "The New Biography," 109; "Phases of Fiction," 70, 72

"Great Men's Houses" (Woolf), 28

Hardy, Thomas, 33–34

"Haworth, November 1904" (Woolf), 28

Hogarth Press, 24, 56, 58–59, 117, 120

Homer, 40–41

"Hours, The" (Woolf), 85–86

"Hours in a Library" (Woolf), 107

Hussey, Mark, 87

Jacob's Room (Woolf), 56, 86, 94

Joyce, James, 41

Keats, John, 35, 62
King Lear (Shakespeare), 47

Leaska, Mitchell, 77
Lee, Hermione, 79, 137
Lehmann, John, 59
Letters of Virginia Woolf: Vol. III, 40, 60, 69, 121; Vol. V, 40, 60, 63, 120; Vol. VI, 29
Life and Last Words of Wilfrid Ewart (Ewart), 109
"Life Itself" (Woolf), 110
London Scene, The (Woolf), 26
"London Scene, The" (Woolf), 27

Macaulay, Rose, 60
Mansfield, Katherine, 58
memoir, 106–9
Moment and Other Essays, The (Woolf): "The Art of Fiction," 32; "The Faery Queen," 60; "The Leaning Tower," 30, 33, 45, 46, 47, 48, 81
Moments of Being (Woolf), 54, 106, 108
Mrs. Dalloway (Woolf), 16, 33, 41, 43, 44, 57, 77, 86; character development,, 85 94, 95, 97, 101, 119; conflict in, 89–90, 92, 93; structure, 87; "tinselly" problem, 96; working title, "The Hours", 85–86

Mrs. Dalloway's Party: A Short Story Sequence (Woolf; McNichold, ed.): "Mrs. Dalloway in Bond St.," 125

Noble, Joan Russell, 5, 78, 120
nonfiction sparks: biography, 109–12; essay, 112–19; memoir, 106–9; novel, 69–73, 76
novelists, 67–68, 72

Odyssey (Homer), 40–41, 43
Oldfield, Sybil, 78
Orlando (Woolf), 33, 57, 77, 97, 98, 109, 111

Partigers, The (Woolf), 20, 73
poetry, 59–63, 64, 65, 82, 121–29
poetry sparks, 120–29; characters, 125–27; experiments, satire, comedy, revolt, memory, 127–29; the senses and the world, 123–25; starting, 121–23
publishing, 6, 55–61, 63; self-publishing a chapbook, 63–64. See also Hogarth Press

Recollections of Virginia Woolf (Noble, ed.), 5, 78, 120
"Reminiscences" (Woolf), 107

Rilke, Rainer Maria, 58

Room of One's Own, A (Woolf), 4, 6, 9, 19, 20, 23, 29, 33, 41, 48, 50, 72, 77–78, 114, 116, 118, 127, 129

Sackville-West, Vita, 64, 111

Second Common Reader, The (Woolf): "How Should One Read a Book?," 45, 51, 119; "Two Parsons," 110

setting, 102–3

Shakespeare, William, 34, 47, 51, 54, 61, 62, 97

Shelley, Percy, 63

"Sketch of the Past, A" (Woolf), 53, 106

Spender, Stephen, 59

Stape, J. H., 60

Stephen, Julia, 46, 53, 108

Stephen, Sir Leslie, 46–47, 108

Strachey, Lytton, 109

stream of consciousness, 29–30, 37

structure, 87–88

"Summing Up, A" (Woolf), 122

Thoreau, Henry David, 34

Three Guineas (Woolf), 114, 117

Tolstoy, Leo, 58

To the Lighthouse (Woolf), 15–16, 33, 57, 73, 77, 86, 94, 95, 98, 100, 103; character in, 93–94, 95, 98, 101, 103; interior conflict in, 89; introduction by Mark Hussey, 87; structure, 87–88; "Time Passes," 65; "We perish, each alone," 103; "The Window," 88, 104–5

Turgenev, Ivan, 89

Ulysses (Joyce), 41, 43

Virginia Woolf (Lee), 79, 137

Virginia Woolf (Webb), 79

Virginia Woolf: A Biography (Q. Bell), 79

Virginia Woolf: The Complete Shorter Fiction (Dick, ed.)

Virginia Woolf: Interviews and Recollections (Stape, ed.), 60, 78

Virginia Woolf: A Writer's Life (Gordon), 46, 79

Virginia Woolf Reader, The (Leaska, ed.), 77; "The Mark on the Wall," 123

Voyage Out, The (Woolf), 43–44

Waste Land, The (Eliot), 58–59

Waves, The (Woolf), 33

Webb, Ruth, 79

West, Rebecca, 58, 78

Women and Writing (Barrett), 78

Woolf, Leonard, 24–25, 56, 58, 78, 117

Woolf, Virginia: advice for writers, 6, 33–34, 55, 71–73, 81; advice on dialogue, 104; advice on poetry writing, 61–63, 64, 65, 82, 121–29; advice on publishing, 6, 55–61, 63; advice to readers, 45–52; on apprenticeship, 55–57; author's vision and, 6, 33, 57; as best-selling author, 33, 57; Bloomsbury Thursdays, 5, 84–85; body of work, 11, 50–51; on character, 62, 70–71, 96; childhood, 46, 53, 107, 108; conditions necessary to produce a work of art, 9–16; diary keeping, 13–18, 51, 85; on dissecting fiction, 30–32; dog, Pinka, 41; on doubting, 72–73; education, 46; on essay writing, 48–51, 112–19; finding her own voice, 56; first novel of, 56; first paid review, 22; five hundred a year, 19, 23–24, 137; on her own working space, 23–26 (see also Room of One's Own, A); Hogarth Press and, 56, 58–59, 117, 120; home in Tavistock Square, 24; house in Gordon Square, Bloomsbury, 24; importance of the creative life, 7; inheritance, 19–20; instinct for beginnings, 86; on journalism, 22–23, 28, 50–51; killing the Angel in the House, 12; "a little spark of fire," 67–68; on memoirs, 47–48, 106–9; at Monk's House, 4, 25, 41; on the novel, 69–73; on the novelist, 67–68, 72; personality and habits, 3–4, 10, 17, 22, 27; on plots, 87; "poet's prose" and, 59–60; on reviews and reviewers, 34–35; scene building, 88; story structure, 87–88; stream of consciousness, 29–30, 37; visit to the Brontë parsonage, 24; on walking or rambling, 39–42; on writers' homes and writing spaces, 24–25, 27; writing habits, 10–11, 69, 84, 85–86

Writer's Diary, A: Being Extracts from the Diary of Virginia Woolf (L. Woolf, ed.), 13, 15, 16, 40, 51, 56, 57, 58, 65, 72, 78, 85, 87, 88, 89, 93, 96

Years, The (Woolf), 33
Yeats, W. B., 120

PERMISSIONS